The Power of the Whole

The Power of the Whole

What Is Lost by Focusing on Individual Things

Sean Slade

ROWMAN & LITTLEFIELD
Lanham • Boulder • New York • London

Published by Rowman & Littlefield
An imprint of The Rowman & Littlefield Publishing Group, Inc.
4501 Forbes Boulevard, Suite 200, Lanham, Maryland 20706
www.rowman.com

86-90 Paul Street, London EC2A 4NE, United Kingdom

Copyright © 2024 by Sean Slade

All rights reserved. No part of this book may be reproduced in any form or by any electronic or mechanical means, including information storage and retrieval systems, without written permission from the publisher, except by a reviewer who may quote passages in a review.

British Library Cataloguing in Publication Information Available

Library of Congress Cataloging-in-Publication Data Available

ISBN 9781475873665 (cloth) | ISBN 9781475873672 (paper) | ISBN 9781475873689 (ebook)

Contents

Foreword	vii
Preface	ix
PART I: THE WHOLE BIG PICTURE	**1**
1 It's All Connected	3
Interconnectedness and Interactions	4
Intra-connectedness and Reactions	5
2 The Myopic View	11
Can't See the Forest for the Trees	11
Can't See the Neighborhood for the Houses	17
PART II: THE WHOLE OF EDUCATION	**27**
3 The Whole Approach	29
Back-to-Basics or Fostering Synergy?	29
Wholeness, Interconnectedness, and Education	33
Moving away from the Myopic and toward the Whole	36
Focusing on the Purpose	37
Educational Hoarders	40
4 A Whole Education	45
Hidden Curriculum	45
Socially and Emotionally	49
The Absence of a Core Reason	53
Finland and the End of Subjects	56

5	From the Whole Child to the Whole Community	61
	It Often Starts with Health but Ends with Education	61
	Whole Child	64
	Whole School	71
	Whole Community	75
6	Health, Government, and the World	81
	Whole Health	81
	Whole Government	84
	Whole World	86

PART III: WHOLENESS AND WHAT TO DO   **91**

7	How It Happens	93
	PBL, Service Learning, and Taking the Broader View	93
	Whole-Part-Whole	97
	Commonality of Objective and Mindset	99
8	A Collaborative, Collective Focus	103
	Weaving	106
	Networks and Working Those Nets	107
9	The Whole Is Greater than the Sum of Its Parts	115

Bibliography   117

About the Author   127

Foreword

We often seek to transform education by looking intently at it internally—its subjects, content, and its standards. We rarely look at the bigger picture or the external world outside of education. Yet there is a lot to learn from our broader world—its connections and interconnections—to see what we can learn from it about our education systems.

This book, by my colleague, friend, and long-distance hiking partner Sean Slade, does just that. It seeks to learn from the world around us to understand what we can apply to education. It is a conscious effort for us to work smarter, not just harder.

Sean has given almost all his professional life to supporting young people and their identities in the fullness of who they are—not as sliced and diced test scores and accountability judgments, on the one hand, nor as boxes to be ticked and categories to be filled by identity politics, on the other. We are all multitudes, as Walt Whitman said, and dealing, as an educator, with any child or young person in ways that do not try to get to grips with how rounded they are, and how well-rounded they might become, is an insult to their dignity as human beings.

For decades, pursuing a whole child philosophy went against the grain of educational policy priorities in nations across the world—priorities that favored standardized testing, curriculum prescription, top-down accountability, and technological quick fixes that reduced the costs of teaching instead. Despite its classical and credible historical roots, paying attention to the whole person in their whole environment, as a whole school, has been given short shrift. Our students have been disconnected from their learning, their world, and themselves in the chase after grade point averages and prospects of quick success. It is time for us to turn disconnection into interconnection.

Everything is connected to everything else. It is true of our world and its many ecosystems, and it is true of our education systems. Things are not isolated, and we rarely thrive in isolation. By taking the broader view—a more holistic view of what we are seeking—we are able to better understand how our education ecosystem fits (or too often doesn't) together. This book aims to change our perspective on education by first focusing on what is around all of us, our world, our communities, and our neighborhoods and their interconnections. It then takes this same focus on education and its inherent ecosystems.

Things are changing. We have moved on from an obsession with test scores and accountability, and we are seeing more holistic approaches to education. Terms like "Whole School," "Whole Community," and "Whole Child" are more commonplace. There are changes afoot outside of education too—Whole Person, Whole Health, Whole of Government are all recent approaches to better understand and appreciate how we are connected and interconnected.

Such holistic, or whole-istic, approaches do not need a whole load of new money. They just need new mindsets. They need the courage of most educators' existing convictions about what's right and best for our kids. If you're ready to step forward and be part of this movement, this book is a great place to start.

Andy Hargreaves
Ottawa
August 2023

Preface

We have a habit of raising individual *things* up in importance at the expense of ignoring the *whole* big picture. We have become somewhat myopic toward *things* that do not justify attention while forgetting the reason we are doing something in the first place. We have been focusing more on individual items and metrics while taking our eye off the ball of the whole reason why we are educating in the first place. We have been ignoring the power of the whole, both in reason and in process.

This book is designed for educators who question how and why we do things in education. This is not designed only for school leaders, nor is it only for teachers. This book seeks to take a broader look at our world—the world around us, and outside our classroom doors, and then apply it to our education system. It seeks to take the bigger picture of what we are trying to achieve, how we are or aren't achieving that, and how we can start to make changes.

The book is divided into parts each focusing on a different theme. Part I outlines the power of interconnectedness and wholeness in the broader world—from nature to our neighborhoods. Part II focuses on why we must take a more whole-istic approach to education in particular. Part III focuses on how we can do this more and utilize the power of the whole to the educational process and the sector. Overall the book asks the following questions:

- What can we learn from the world around us?
- What can be infused into education?
- How can we be smarter, not just work the same but harder?

Education, while a morally rich sector and profession, too often allows habit, and the status quo, to dictate its processes and restrict its progress. We are quick to ignore some simple truths that are quite apparent in the noneducation world. We are not the only sector or profession to do this, but we are one of the most influential professions, precisely because we help develop people for their future. As such, changing education changes the trajectory of the world.

PART I: THE WHOLE BIG PICTURE

We look directly at the broader world and highlight how interconnected it is. Changes in one area affect another—or more often all others. Whether it is the introduction of a new species into an ecosystem or the effects of a new drug, there is overwhelming evidence of our connectedness and interconnectedness. We cannot and must not view *things* in isolation.

PART II: THE WHOLE OF EDUCATION

We take this approach to our sector, education, and unpack what it could and should mean for us and the profession. When we introduce a new *thing*—a policy, a new testing apparatus, or a new metric—we often change what education is, and we too frequently do it without considering the broader ramifications. We can inadvertently change what education is for, how it is delivered, and ultimately, we can change its purpose and value. Since the turn of the century, with a myopic focus on standardized testing in a select number of core subjects, education has become less about developing citizens ready for society and more about developing test-takers. We have reduced the process and meaning of education, and, at the same time, we have become blinkered to how these content areas fit together. We have grown ignorant of the interconnectedness between *things* in education.

We are changing though. There has been a shift in our educational psyche toward a more whole-istic approach in recent years. Whether it be a growing appreciation of a Whole Child approach to education, which seeks to develop the student socially, emotionally, mentally, physically, as well as cognitively, or whether it be a renewed appreciation of the symbiotic link between health and education, there are changes happening.

PART III: WHOLENESS AND WHAT TO DO

In the final part, we look at how we can better incorporate such a whole-istic approach into our education processes and ultimately our system. For many, it starts with just changing our mindsets—understanding why we teach and for what purpose.

We are learning from each other, we are networking, and we are sharing strategies and we are connecting. We are demonstrating that we as a profession are interconnected and we can do better by appreciating our wholeness.

This book is about ourselves and our world, but it is also a book about education. Education is undergoing constant scrutiny—as it should. It is also being dissected, sliced, and diced, slivers being reviewed under a microscope while other aspects are left ignored or worse discarded and forgotten. What makes, or made, an education successful is too often left behind in the shadows when we focus too closely on what we think should be in the spotlight.

It is the author's belief that we are entering a period of time when relooking at how these *things* interact and intersect will be pertinent to their and our success. Whether we call it the intersection of subjects, or the hidden curriculum, whether we frame it by the project-based or service-learning moniker, or whether we view it as an encompassing system of support, we are in essence talking about the same thing—how we make something whole again after so many years of dissecting it into pieces. It is the glue that holds *things* together, that makes sense of the various actions and learning that we engage in. Without a bigger picture view—a whole view—many of our actions have become individualized, separate from their connection, separated from their meaning, and divorced of value. They become actions and activities for the sake of themselves only.

It is time to use the power of the whole and take in the big picture.

PART I
THE WHOLE BIG PICTURE

Chapter 1

It's All Connected

We have spent decades focusing on the specifics of each skill, segment, sector, and system. We have pinpointed how each can be defined, and dissected, so that we understand and appreciate the individuality of each. We have spent countless hours homing in on each as a finite set of attributes in order to perfect that one *thing*.

But what we are now realizing is what we have lost of how these *things* work together.

We have lost how they complement and support each other.

We have lost an understanding of what makes these *things* whole.

We have lost and continue to lose the glue that holds these parts together and that is often necessary for the whole to function properly.

We have focused and then siloed *things* across our systems and communities to the point where we are losing what made or makes them beneficial in the first place. We are surrounded by interconnection and symbiosis, everywhere, everyday. We frequently take these things for granted or more often don't even realize they exist because they are so intertwined with our world and our ongoing existence. We only seem to be made aware of these interconnections when we disturb and disrupt them—and the same is true of our man-made systems. The more we dissect and disassemble, the more we realize that we truly don't appreciate the wholeness of what we have.

When we focus on individual actions and individual issues, we can lose sight of the bigger picture. It's that proverbial can't see the forest for the trees. We focus intently on what's in front of us without seeing what's around us.

But we can also lose sight of how the individual parts rely on each other to work effectively. The doctor who specializes in ear, nose, and throat will often need to bring in experts in pulmonary care, allergy treatment, or even dietitians. The body acts as our own primary and personal example of how we need the parts working together to work well. And too often we only realize the interconnectedness when we lose the ability of part of our body or its functions.

Smell is aligned to taste, which is aligned to hunger, motivation, attitude, and desire. Depression is likewise aligned to sleep, energy, physical activity, pain, or a proneness to illness. Throughout history, we have seen examples of how adding a new drug or treatment may cure what's in front of us but harms the body in other ways.

INTERCONNECTEDNESS AND INTERACTIONS

We are interconnected to ourselves and to our ecosystems. When we affect one part of it, we may produce some beneficial outcomes, but frequently we do unexpected harm. Or when we change the ecosystem—local and global—we can unwittingly launch a range of subsequent consequences.

A recent and obscure example of this is the monogamous mating habits of albatrosses and climate change. Two seemingly unconnected issues yet interconnected and co-influential. As reported by Tess McClure in *The Guardian*[1] in 2021, albatrosses typically are monogamous birds mating with one partner for life. These "marriages" or relationships have practical purposes as the pair typically shares duties that include seeking food—an ordeal that can sometimes take months and, by some reports, several thousands of miles—and taking on egg incubation duties. Pairs typically will return to each other annually, perform the same mating ritual, and resume where they left off.

However, all is not right in the albatross world and climate change is seemingly upending this relationship. In a new Royal Society study released in 2021, researchers claim that climate change and warming waters are pushing black-browed albatross break-up or "divorce" rates higher. The typical "divorce" rate of albatross pairs is only between 1 and 3 percent with the vast majority remaining with their lifetime partners. But in the years with unusually warm water temperatures that has risen to 8 percent. That may not seem like a huge jump, but it's up to an 800 percent increase from the norm.

Climate change and divorce. What could be unwittingly and unexpectedly causing this? How are these two *things* possibly connected? The theories range but two of the most commonsensical are that rising temperatures have caused changes to fish numbers which in turn was causing the birds to hunt for longer and fly further. If birds then failed to return for a breeding season, their partners often move on with someone new.

The other suggested reason is that as the waters get warmer and the environments change making life generally more difficult, the albatrosses' stress hormones go up. Stress hormones don't play well with reproduction and this failure to reproduce may be seen by some albatrosses as a sound reason to find a new mate.

Whatever the definitive reason or reasons it appears likely that climate change and warming waters in particular are causing changes to their mating habits. And this is what we can see or view via research. The impact of warming waters would surely extend beyond just affecting the marriage success of albatrosses and impact a vast range of species, behaviors, actions, and reactions, because we are interconnected with our ecosystem and our environment.

How do the relationship habits of albatrosses relate to our ongoing and needed education reform debate? They don't. Or they don't via any direct link. The purpose here and at the start of this book is to illustrate how our world, and our worlds inside that greater world, are interconnected. Seeing or viewing things in isolation is folly and can lead us to flawed understanding, inadequate assumptions, and false conclusions. It can also lead us to decisions that do more harm than good, even though the initial judgment appeared sound and the intent was positive.

There are of course more tragic examples of interconnectedness than that of the albatross. Times when the outcomes were not just altering to behavior but devastating. We have seen this in the unintended outcomes of numerous medications introduced over the decades. One of the worst examples of this was the Thalidomide tragedy of the late 1950s and early 1960s that has been cited as the "biggest man-made medical disaster ever,"[2] but it is by no means the only one. And as is often the case when we delve into how we are connected and interconnected there are also positive benefits of drugs that cause major issues, even thalidomide. The drug is still being used in parts of the world to treat myeloma, Crohn's disease, multiple sclerosis, and leprosy—though not for pregnant women.

It's all connected, and for too many years we have ignored the interconnectedness of *things*. The introduction into a system or an ecosystem of a new entity, chemical, or organism will often substantially affect that ecosystem because it is interconnected. This interconnectedness goes both ways of course. There are negative outcomes and there are positive or bonus outcomes—and of course, there are many examples where a change in an ecosystem brings both positive and negative effects.

INTRA-CONNECTEDNESS AND REACTIONS

Take a look at your latest or most recent prescription drug. The list of possible side effects will typically—at least here in the United States—go on for one, two sometimes three pages. What this is highlighting is a number of things—the interplay between the new drug and its ecosystem (in this case your body); the variation or differentiation of potential effects (each ecosystem is somewhat different); and our general lack of understanding of how and where these effects may occur. Such side effects can be physical—headaches, nausea, aches, and pains; it can be cognitive—lack of clarity, foggy mind, loss of memory; or it can be emotional—anxiety, depression. There is a broad range of potential side effects of our interconnectedness and what may occur can be varied.

Yet our understanding of such interconnectedness is based more on watching for reactions rather than anticipating potential outcomes. We base our understanding less on knowing what side effects will occur than on testing, trialing a new drug, and waiting to see what things happen. In terms of understanding interconnectedness, we are still very much in the infancy. We at still discovering how and where something will affect something else though we are further along from where we were a century or more earlier.

The thalidomide disaster also had the effect of making the U.S. Federal Drug Administration (FDA) more stringent on passing or refusing medications and on listing out the many (many!) potential reactions that patients may experience. Since 2012 the FDA has recalled over 13,000 drugs and while not everyone is due to adverse side effects, they do account for a fair proportion of recalls. According to the FDA, "a drug recall is the most effective way to protect the public from a defective or potentially harmful product. A recall is a voluntary action taken by a company at any time to remove a defective drug product from the market."[3] The drug is typically removed from the market when its risks outweigh its benefits—there may be safety issues with the drug, including unintended side effects and reactions. The FDA also takes into account the number of people taking a drug being considered for removal so as to not harm those patients.

A Yale School of Medicine report released in 2017[4] found that nearly a third of medications approved from 2001 through 2010 had major safety issues years after they had been approved and made widely available to patients. This was further reported out by numerous news outlets including National Public Radio (NPR).[5]

Seventy-one of the 222 drugs approved in the first decade of the millennium were withdrawn, required a "black box" warning on side effects, or warranted a safety announcement about new risks, Dr. Joseph Ross, an associate professor of medicine at Yale School of Medicine, and colleagues reported in JAMA *on Tuesday. The study included safety actions through Feb. 28.*

"While the administration pushes for less regulation and faster approvals, those decisions have consequences," Ross says. The Yale researchers' previous studies concluded that the FDA approves drugs faster than its counterpart

agency in Europe does and that the majority of pivotal trials in drug approvals involved fewer than 1,000 patients and lasted six months or less.

It took a median of 4.2 years after the drugs were approved for these safety concerns to come to light, the study found, and issues were more common among psychiatric drugs, biologic drugs, drugs that were granted "accelerated approval" and drugs that were approved near the regulatory deadline for approval.

The issue being raised here isn't with the FDA and their approval or withdrawal process but rather the interconnectedness of *things* that are all around us. This is only increased as more people take more medicines and the possible number of interactions increases. Drug A may not have adverse side effects when combined in the body with drug B, but it may well be a different story when it's A + (B + C).

A + B = ☺
A + (B + C) = 😐
A + (B + C) x F + J + P + X = 😵 😄 😖

But we don't only have to realize that these *things* are interrelated when they break or go wrong and start a vicious cycle. We can also focus on the way they interact and heighten the benefits we get out of each one and begin a virtuous cycle. We've highlighted previously the adverse effect of medication on the body but sometimes—unfortunately, less frequently—we find that they produce an unintended positive or bonus effect on the body.

Ecstasy, or MDMA (methylenedioxymethamphetamine), was first developed in 1912 by a German company as a compound drug to help synthesize medications that control bleeding, though its use and misuse has expanded considerably since then to include marriage counseling, post-traumatic stress disorder or PTSD, depression, and of course as a recreational rave drug most notably in the 1980s and 1990s. While it was legally prescribed during the early twentieth century, its use as a mood enhancer wasn't truly understood and utilized until the 1970s when many psychiatrists, psychologists, and counselors found it beneficial to patients who were needing to get in touch with their emotions. This included psychiatrists treating child abuse, trauma, and what we now term PTSD. In the 1950s, it was also reported to have been trialed as a truth serum by the CIA though found to be unreliable.

Through the 1970s and up to the 1980s, it was considered effective and was legally prescribed as a way to have breakthrough conversations and tap into the patient's emotions often dramatically reducing the amount of time for treatment and counseling to work.

MDMA-assisted couple therapy was conducted in the 1970s and 1980s being shown to be beneficial to couples taking part in therapy, finding that it reduced fear of emotional hurt and improved communication and introspection. In the article "Couple Therapy with MDMA—Proposed Pathways of Action," Anne Wagner expanded on these findings.

> *MDMA's empathogenic qualities have made it a prime candidate as an adjunct to psychotherapy. When considering the couple therapy context, understanding the neurochemical experience related to romantic love illuminates this potentially catalytic combination. The hormones and neurotransmitters most closely associated with the experience of love include oxytocin and vasopressin (linking to attachment and bonding), dopamine and serotonin (causing pleasure and positive mood), and the brain areas most impacted include the amygdala (registering threat, happiness, and fear), prefrontal cortex (related to reasoning) and the hippocampus (engagement with thoughts and memories), as well as the caudate nucleus (registering love) and the hypothalamus (registering lust).*[6]

As with many legal drugs it was then used outside counseling and clinical settings as users sought the experience of pleasure that MDMA can produce. And once it was banned, and made illegal, its use skyrocketed.

The drug became a street drug in the burgeoning rave and nightclub scenes and was outlawed in 1985 as part of the U.S. government's "War on Drugs" and then likely as a consequence of the banning, the media's portrayal, and the increased awareness, it ballooned in popularity via the drug's newfound illegal status. Somewhat ironically the drug which had been used for decades as a mood enhancer and release for trauma victims was deemed to have no real medicinal value but a high potential for abuse. This classification moved MDMA, or Ecstasy, or Molly, from the psychiatrist's cabinet to the jean pocket of many teenagers and young adults overnight.

Since 1985 there has been an ongoing battle between the risks of the street drug Ecstasy and the beneficial effects of MDMA for treating trauma and PTSD especially—including military combat, sexual assault, and childhood abuse. The drug has received "breakthrough therapy designation"[7] by the Food and Drug Administration (FDA) in the United States, but currently only when aligned with talk therapy.

Here is a drug that was designed to be a compound for helping control bleeding and that was then found to be extremely beneficial in something totally unaligned—treating emotions and aiding with counseling. It has been used by psychiatrists, psychologists, and counselors, to help those suffering from abuse, trauma, and PTSD, and then ultimately by ravers to enhance their experience. This drug to stop bleeding has gone to the psychiatrist's couch, to the battlefield, to the nightclubs. It has gone from a blood halter to a marriage saver and then a party raver.

It has been discussed in the confines of the CIA, debated in the chambers on Capitol Hill, and very likely used in every nightclub around the world.

This is not to debate its worth or its merits but rather to (again) point out that what we often see as a single entity with a single outcome can and frequently does have a multitude of effects.

Invent a drug to help bleeding and watch it become the biggest party drug of the 1980s.

The bottom line here is that we are connected and interconnected and too often when we try to prize or isolate one part of the puzzle it impacts parts we never thought of or knew existed.

And the second truth is that the most obvious incidents of us not truly understanding the ecosystemic nature of, well, nature are frequently the incidents where things go wrong. There are examples in medicine and there are examples in nature itself.

And for whatever reason, several of the examples come from my homeland Australia where a number of European or Central American species were introduced—often for food or recreational purposes such as hunting—and subsequently ran amok. Even in some of the cases where new species were introduced for the reason of curtailing or restricting another species, the consequences were frequently disastrous.

NOTES

1. McClure, T., *Climate Crisis Pushes Albatross "Divorce" Rates Higher—Study*, The Guardian, November 24, 2021. Retrieved December 8, 2023, from https://www.theguardian.com/environment/2021/nov/24/climate-crisis-pushes-albatross-divorce-rates-higher-study.

2. Fan, R., *Thalidomide: "The Biggest Man-Made Medical Disaster Ever,"* Medium, August 3, 2021. Retrieved January 8, 2023, from https://medium.com/frame-of-reference/thalidomide-the-biggest-man-made-medical-disaster-ever-2988096e7716.

3. Center for Drug Evaluation and Research, *Drug Recalls*, U.S. Food and Drug Administration, n.d. Retrieved January 8, 2023, from https://www.fda.gov/drugs/drug-safety-and-availability/drug-recalls.

4. Nicholas, S., & Downing, M. D., *Postmarket Safety Events among Therapeutics Approved by the FDA*, JAMA, May 9, 2017. Retrieved January 8, 2023, from https://jamanetwork.com/journals/jama/fullarticle/2625319.

5. Lupkin, S., *One-Third of New Drugs Had Safety Problems after FDA Approval*, NPR, May 9, 2017. Retrieved January 8, 2023, from https://www.npr.org/sections/health-shots/2017/05/09/527575055/one-third-of-new-drugs-had-safety-problems-after-fda-approval.

6. Wagner, A. C., *Couple Therapy with MDMA—Proposed Pathways of Action*, Frontiers in Psychology, 12, 2021, https://doi.org/10.3389/fpsyg.2021.733456.

7. Zagorski, N., *Psychedelic Therapy Hits Another Milestone, But Caution Urged*, Psychiatric News, July 22, 2021. Retrieved January 8, 2023, from https://psychnews.psychiatryonline.org/doi/10.1176/appi.pn.2021.7.14.

Chapter 2

The Myopic View

CAN'T SEE THE FOREST FOR THE TREES

The examples of interconnectedness can also be seen—frequently more often—in review. We have consistently tampered with, introduced into, and generally ignored the interplay of ecosystems we have found ourselves in.

There was definitely a cavalier-to-arrogant attitude in the way that new species were introduced to what many assumed were new lands. Cavalier in not appreciating the new lands and their own biodiversity. Arrogant in dismissing the indigenous population—their enduring relationship and understanding of the land, its fauna, and flora. And willfully or gleefully ignorant in assumptions and actions—perhaps because of the recent nineteenth-century discoveries in science that allowed many Europeans to assume that they knew it all or at least enough. What we have found out since the introduction of species is that they/we knew enough just to be dangerous. And frequently very dangerous.

The fox had been released several times for hunting purposes before, but the introduction of a new species doesn't always work out as planned. It is a new environment with new ecosystems and sometimes the new arrival doesn't always cope as intended. And it wasn't until a more concerted and planned effort by a wealthy landowner in rural Victoria, Australia, that their population truly began to flourish. As Christopher Johnson, a professor of wildlife conservation at the University of Tasmania, explains,

> *Some early releases were evidently quite serious attempts to establish wild populations, such as a liberation of a group of at least six foxes in the Dandenong Ranges in 1864. Released animals were rarely, if ever, seen again. They may have been killed by hunters or dingoes, or they might have taken poison baits*

that were laid for dingoes and stray dogs. In any case, they did not establish viable populations. It was not until about 1874 that a fox population finally took off, on the Werribee Park property of the wealthy Chirnside family. From that point the fox was unstoppable. Despite all attempts at control, it swept like an avenging fire through all of the southern half of Australia in just a few decades.[1]

Within one hundred years, the fox had spread across most of Australia, including all of southern Australia and even Tasmania—250 kilometers (or 155 miles) to the south by sea. It seems only the tropical temperature of the north has stopped them from expanding their territory and dominance. Tasmania was not able to remain fox-free as they were also deliberately introduced, and eradication efforts remain in effect. The "Global Invasive Species Database"[2] cites that the European foxes are considered a threat to fourteen bird species, forty-eight mammals, twelve reptiles, and two amphibians listed under the Environmental Protection and Biodiversity Conservation Act 1999.

The cost of the reported seven-million-strong fox population in Australia on the environment and agricultural industries has been listed at more than $227 million.[3] Quite a lot of impact for one species, though this wasn't the only invasive species to impact Australia, and nor was it the only time a new species was introduced without considering the larger view impact.

The introduction of rabbits, also for hunting, echoed, and then surpassed that of the foxes. "The introduction of a few rabbits could do little harm and might provide a touch of home, in addition to a spot of hunting," said Thomas Austin, rather audaciously, in 1859. Upon arriving in Australia, Austin asked his nephew in England to send him "12 grey rabbits, five hares, 72 partridges, and some sparrows"[4] so he could continue his hobby of hunting. As a result, and due to the prolificity of the rabbit and the ideal conditions in this country, this led to a rabbit population explosion that had a devastating effect on Australia's ecology. They are suspected of being the most significant known factor in species and plant loss and erosion problems in Australia. Change or introduce one thing and you may likely change a lot more than expected.

And then there is the infamous cane toad.

The introduction of the cane toad was at least rational, though shortsighted. Their introduction was not because of some wealthy landowner's pastime or desire to be more British, but rather an attempt to eradicate another pest—the French's Cane Beetle and the Greyback Cane Beetle—which were in the process of decimating the northeastern state of Queensland's sugar cane crops. This was an attempt of using one species to decimate another, but the ultimate outcome was far from successful.

Following the apparent success of the cane toad in eating the beetles threatening the sugarcane plantations of Puerto Rico, Hawaii, and the Philippines, a similar push was made to release the toad in Australia.

Just over one hundred cane toads were transported and eventually released into the sugar cane fields in 1935. To their credit, the Commonwealth Department of Health at the time decided to halt any future introductions so as to study what implications this mighty group of one hundred would do. Unfortunately, the die was cast, and the damage is felt to this day. By 1936 the study was complete and in 1937 another 62,000 toadlets had been released into the wild. The original group had increased into tens if not hundreds of thousands and with this next release, the toads became firmly established in Queensland, increasing exponentially.

As was reported in the Overstaying Their Welcome: Cane Toads in Australia by Tina Butler,

> The plan backfired completely and absolutely. As it turns out, cane toads cannot jump very high, only about two feet actually, so they did not eat the beetles that for the most part lived in the upper stalks of cane plants. Instead of going after the beetles, as growers had planned, the cane toads began going after everything else in sight—insects, bird's eggs, and even native frogs. And because the toads are poisonous, they began to kill would-be predators. The toll on native species has been immense.[5]

To make matters worse, it was soon discovered that cane toads emit a poison from their skin so even when potential predators come across them, they are quickly extinguished. Fish that consume the cane toad eggs die. Animals both native and non-native that catch and eat the cane toads die. And this includes other poisonous or dangerous Australian animals including the freshwater crocodiles, tiger snakes, red-bellied black snakes, death adders, and dingoes. The cane toad dies but the predator also dies. What keeps their population growing is the large number of eggs that the female lays—between 8,000 and 35,000 at a time—though only 0.5 percent survive through to maturity.

Cane toad populations have exploded, and they now span Queensland, the Northern Territory, and even into Western Australia, some 3,000 kilometers, or 2,000 miles, from where they were first introduced. And as they have multiplied and migrated, they have decimated local fauna. The population of a number of native predatory reptiles has declined, including monitor lizards, various species of snakes, and crocodiles. In contrast, the beetles that caused the toads to be imported remained unaffected until a chemical pesticide was developed.

It seems that the only ones to experience any beneficial effect from this invasive species introduction—though that is debatable—have been pets and some humans licking the toads for hallucinogenic effects, though this won't dent the toad population.

This was how Jodie Munro O'Brien of the *Courier Mail* described it in her article: "It's a dog of a way to get high but Queensland pooches are lapping up hallucinogenic sweat from cane toads."

Queensland dogs are getting addicted to the hallucinogenic sweat that oozes off the backs of cane toads. Vets warn that some dogs are so desperate for a fix they deliberately hunt down the amphibians to stimulate the excretion of the deadly poison, then lick their prey. Like all addicts, the pooches are risking their lives for their cheap thrill.[6]

These are somewhat obvious or directly linked outcomes of introduction. We also see outcomes when parts of our ecosystem are taken away, without truly understanding their broad role and place in complex ecosystems.

Our own local and global environments are ecosystems that function, adjust, and adapt on a constant and consistent basis. A change here evokes another change there, and the reason is because we are connected and interconnected.

Trees provide us shade, fruit, beauty, and oxygen. But their benefits extend beyond what we can use them for or build out of them and into and across our lives. Just as their roots expand into and across subterranean spaces hidden from our view their influence often is broad, diverse, and hidden. More often than not they also provide us with unexpected benefits or bonuses and frequently ones that we don't or didn't initially realize.

From a big-picture view, there is nothing more grand, and grandiose, than the Amazon Rainforest and its effects on the rest of the world.

Everything is interconnected. In the Amazon—which spans an area comparable to the contiguous United States—there are no spare parts, so it is not a matter of focusing on a specific area or certain species. Natural cycles are being altered, tipping a delicate balance that affects local, regional, and even global levels and getting closer and closer to a point of no return. At the current rates of destruction, that's 20 years away at most.

—The Amazon Approaches Its Tipping Point, The Nature Conservancy[7]

Spanning a greater surface area than the continental US or Western Europe, it has frequently been described as the *lungs of the world*[8] cleaning and recycling the air, taking in carbon dioxide and releasing oxygen at incredible amounts. The forest comprises 10 percent of all biomass on Earth, and acts as a giant sponge, absorbing and storing massive amounts of carbon dioxide while emitting up to 20 percent of the Earth's oxygen.

But more recently, the Amazon has also taken on a new moniker the *heart of the world*.[9] It helps drive weather, pumping water vapor around the world. Millions of trees acting in combination serve as a pump sending water vapor into the air creating rivers of vapor that then circumnavigate the globe, influencing and affecting weather.

The Amazon rainforest draws water from the ground and releases the moisture into the atmosphere through a process called transpiration. Transpiration is evaporation, but it is the evaporation of water that has gone through the trees. Think of it like blood in our veins—but unlike blood, the tree water is then pushed up into the sky as a kind of water vapor.

—Flying Rivers of the Amazon Rainforest—
A Critical Rain Generator for the Planet, Alexis Lassman[10]

But as we continue to chop down these *lungs* and *heart* of the world we are affecting not only the Amazon Rainforest we are affecting the global weather patterns. These giant rivers in the sky as they have been described by Craig Welch,[11] an environment writer at National Geographic, formed out of the Amazon nourish almost every country in South America and boost the global precipitation pool.

But when trees are cut down, this fundamental balance is disrupted. Fewer trees mean less moisture sticking to leaves and less humidity in the air. Less humidity reduces the amount of rain produced and rather being a virtual cycle where rain that is produced falls again on the rainforest, it becomes a vicious cycle where less rain is produced causing less subsequent rain.

The water supply for millions of people around the world is affected. The rainforest's ability to regenerate and repopulate is affected. And the carbon cycle is also disrupted. Fewer trees take in less carbon dioxide and increase our inability to reduce global warming.

And if the Amazon is too large, or too distant an issue to spark concern, then most of us will likely remember or have read about the hurricane that hit New Orleans in 2005. People stranded on their roofs with SOS signs; entire wards were almost washed away; over $125 billion in damage, and 1800 lives were lost.

The Lower Ninth was inundated 10 years ago when Katrina hit, in large part because of previous wetlands loss. It has still not fully recovered, and it's here where Brad Pitt has established his Make it Right foundation to build sustainable homes.

As the Gulf has gotten warmer, sea levels have risen and land has shrunk. "Louisiana is losing a football field of land an hour. That's one of the fastest rates in the world," said Mack. Wetlands help reduce this land loss as well as protect against hurricane damage.

Most Americans don't realize the importance of Gulf Coast ports. "The mouth of the Mississippi is one of the largest agricultural ports in the U.S. It's also a major port for oil and gas," she said.

—Strategies: Entrepreneurs Preventing the Next Katrina,
Rhonda Abrams[12]

Mangrove depletion, and subsequent mangrove replacement, does more than add or subtract vegetation. Mangroves via their root structure maintain a scaffold to the coastline, restricting sand and soil depletion. They act as a skeleton or as a natural version of the fiber reinforcement inserted inside concrete when buildings are constructed. They hold the structure together and at the same time, their leaves, and branches act to diffuse the power of the flooding, reducing their power and potency.

The wetlands are an ecosystem and its interactions with us, and our systems, are also an ecosystem. What we may assume is just a tree or a shrub can have a greater impact on its surroundings and our way of life than we at first assume.

"Healthy wetlands provide substantial protection against hurricane damage. They reduce surge, store water and slow floodwaters. They also break the waves. The waves are the most damaging to the levees.... Wave energy is like an earthquake,"[13] said Sarah Mack, Ph.D., founder of Tierra Resources, a nonprofit that works with private corporations to come up with new methods of restoring wetlands.

By taking away a barrier and a natural method for diminishing the power of floodwaters these efforts have moved the hurricane's strength closer to New Orleans. Rather than spending millions on efforts that appeared, and intended, to bolster the shipping industry in Louisiana, the state may have been better advised to grow even more mangroves rather than allow their demise. Efforts are underway to replenish the mangroves, yet as often seems to be the case we rush into making changes for short-term wins without carefully considering the broader impacts of our changes and these decisions.

The interconnectedness of the mangroves, the coast, the ecosystem, to trade, shipping, and the survival of New Orleans is not lost on people. We may have been ignorant or oblivious before but now we have clear evidence of the impact that flooding can do and the impact that changes to our ecosystems can bring. As the title of the article states, "New Orleans' Lower 9th Ward is still reeling from Hurricane Katrina's damage 15 years later."

> *Grim hideouts like this one are plentiful across a Lower 9th Ward that 15 years ago became a world symbol for poverty, neglect, and utter devastation, and since has shown few signs of a rebound.*
>
> *Overgrown lots still blanket the landscape in the "backatown" area lakeward of North Claiborne Avenue, where the market for homes has flatlined.*
>
> *As recently as 2018, the neighborhood's population stood at about a third of its pre-Katrina levels, with fewer than 5,000 residents, according to U.S. Census estimates.*
>
> *There were 4,820 households in the Lower 9th Ward in 2000, five years before Katrina. Five years after the storm, the census logged 1,060 households.*

More recent estimates place the number at about 1,675, according to an analysis by The Data Center.[14]

—John Simmerman, NOLA.com

We are starting to understand the impact, or rather impacts, that changes to our ecosystems can make. Introduce a rabbit or a fox for sport and watch an ecosystem be changed forever. Allow the destruction of mangroves to increase shipping and watch as their absence increases the harm that hurricanes bring, affecting the same shipping trade that was being targeted initially. Ecosystems are a series of interconnections, and we have a lot more of them than we first assume or appreciate.

CAN'T SEE THE NEIGHBORHOOD FOR THE HOUSES

The streets where we grew up provided learning experiences, connections, and protections that we weren't always aware of—until we lost them. Our neighborhoods are, and to a certain point were more so, ecosystems where we grew up. The connections formed, the relationships built, and the experiences endured all played into who we were and who we have become.

Our house, in the middle of our street
Our house, in the middle of our
Our house it has a crowd
There's always something happening
And it's usually quite loud.
I remember way back then, when everything was true and when
We would have such a very good time, such a fine time, such a happy time
And I remember how we'd play, simply waste the day away
Then we'd say nothing would come between us, two dreamers

—Our House, Madness, 1982[15]

Many of us recall growing up in streets or neighborhoods where the children were often outside playing, exploring, arguing, cooperating. These streets and these environments were like mini-communities where the skills of teamwork, leadership, decision-making, bargaining were learned as often as the skills of soccer, running, or climbing. These were safe, protected environments where the families would share the lunch table with whoever was present.

This still exists today but unfortunately more sporadically. What is more common now is directed play, or directed learning. Children rarely play in the street or at the local park. Instead, they join a club and are taught skills. It is becoming more commonplace nowadays for children not to have playdates but rather having activities. They are signed up for piano, for soccer, for arts, or for drama classes. Their out-of-school-time activities are organized, scheduled, and based around the premise that there is something to learn. Play for the sake of play itself is in decline.

> *In many schools, playtime is being cut back to make way for extra study time. Increasingly, children's time out of school is also being closely managed on the assumption that this is the best way to cultivate the skills and understanding they need to compete in education and in the workforce. Even parents who believe their children should have a better mix of play styles and more creative, outdoor play often don't make any changes to their daily routines to make it possible. Play just slips off the "to-do" list.*
>
> *A third reason for the decline is fear. Children across the globe spend less time playing outside because parents worry about their safety. These fears may be largely unfounded but they are exacerbated everyday by the relentless, alarmist tendencies of the 24-hour news cycles. Partly for this reason, when children do play outdoors, they are often over supervised by adults, which limits the benefits of playing or even whether children perceive it as real play at all.*
>
> —Pasi Sahlberg and Willian Doyle, Let the Children Play[16]

We have moved on from the *organic socialization* common to many of us Gen Xers to *organized socialization* where activities are planned and frequently objectives set.

This change can be as benign as
We're going to the swimming club, does Jose want to join us?
We thought we'd take them to the movies, has she seen the Marvel film?
Through to
Chaunte, we're signing you up to learn the clarinet.
Swim lessons are three times a week. I'll pick you up straight after school.
And to
You need to learn an instrument—it'll be good for your college resume.

What is currently being learned more so nowadays is the skill and less so the socialization. It is more directed-learning of content or a skill and less self-directed play or discovery. But what have we lost by losing this aspect of growing up? We learn what someone else has deemed important and in doing so also learned abdication of control and choice. This is not necessarily all bad as the skills can be important but what is lost if these are the only or primary forms of socialization is the agency, control, and choice of the individual. Taken out of the activities is the individual's opportunity to have self-direction and to learn by trial and error, as well as the inherent messiness of decision-making, planning, and socialization.

These *organized socialization* activities inadvertently subtract from the experience. No longer are the children themselves organizing. No longer are they creating games, inventing rules, forming teams, or building forts. They rarely, as a consequence, interact with people in their neighborhood who are older/younger/different than themselves and rarely own the activity that they are engaged in.

As we take responsibility for these playdates and lessons away from the child, we take away their ability to own the action. We take away their ability to construct something meaningful for themselves. We take away their ability to invent, try, fail, reinvent. We take away the requirement to be self-sufficient and to be bored.

Hyperfocusing on one thing too often means we lose something that we didn't predict. And then once we realize what we're missing we try and invent a playdate or a lesson to hyper-focus on that element.

How long will it be before we see lessons catering to children's need to socialize or to have unstructured play? We are already seeing vacations marketed as places with no internet access so that we can communicate or even just zone out. Surely the oxymoron of *structured-free-play times* will be next, but we'll probably do it wrong and miss the *whole* point.

> *You Play—the unstructured play sensation. Sign up now for our 6-week course. Between the hours of 4-6 pm and for 3–5-year-olds only. Parents must be present and sign a waiver beforehand. All You Play activities on offer have been planned and vetted by our expert team.*

Pasi Sahlberg and William Doyle's 2020 book Let the Children Play cited earlier in this chapter also provided us with a Foreword from the late Sir Ken Robinson, who echoes these calls to see the myriad of learning and growth opportunities provided through "real play"—play that is free of adult obstruction or direction.

> *These are some of the common characteristics of real play:*
> *It is self-initiated and self-motivated: Real play is freely chosen. If children are forced to play, they may not feel in a state of play at all.*
> *It is creative: Children engage in make-believe that bends reality to accommodate their interests and imagination.*
> *It is active: Real play engages children physically as well as mentally.*
> *It has negotiated rules: The rules of play come from the child, including entry to and from the game and what counts as acceptable behavior within it.*
> *Sahlberg and Doyle cite numerous studies that confirm that real play is essential for a happy childhood and for becoming independent adults. Real*

Chapter 2

play is vital for the physical development of healthy bodies. Growing children need the stimulation that comes from vigorous physical activity, good nutrition, and a safe environment in which to explore their abilities. Real play stimulates children's cognitive development. Children's brains are immensely plastic. Through play, they tap into their natural curiosity and creativity.

Real play helps to form new neural connections in the brain while strengthening existing pathways. Real play facilitates children's emotional development. Through play they explore their personal feelings and ideas and learn how others feel and think. Real play has essential roles in children's social development.[17]

—Foreword by Sir Ken Robinson in Let the Children Play

This is something that many Physical Education teachers and many educators have known for a while. Play, activity, movement are not only good for the body, but it is essential for the mind and the emotional self. A sound Physical Education program is not there to develop athletes but to teach and instill the joy and benefits of movement to every child. It is there to help each child learn more about themselves and what they and their bodies can do. It is there to allow them to learn core skills of cooperation, collaboration, teamwork, perseverance, resilience, decision-making, success, failure, via meaningful, engaging activity.

The social and emotional skills developed through physical education help students create meaningful relationships with their teacher and with each other. Strong relationships built on trust and understanding contribute to a positive school culture . . .

Physical activity provides an opportunity to build character, use teamwork, and foster a sense of belonging in schools. It is important, not only to individual students, but to the overall health of the school community.

—Building School Community through Physical Activity, Eric Nelson[18]

As a Physical Education teacher back in the 1990s, it was something that I strived to focus on—the development of character, of leadership and followship, of learning to cooperate, collaborate and problem solve. PE—note it was never just "Gym"—was more than an avenue to teach sports skills and more than a space to improve health and wellbeing , it was also a great environment to have the child learn more about themselves and the ways they interact with their peers. And there were other great benefits of PE. Besides being health enhancing, it was also an activity that the students took seriously from a personal and social perspective. It mattered how you performed and how you interacted. It also was a great conduit into their "real lives." Make a difference in how they engaged in games during a unit, and they would likely carry that through into the playground. And from the playground into their out-of-school time.

Change the way they thought of themselves or adjust the way they participated and planned games, tactics, problem solving, or team morale, and there was a very good chance that this is the way they behaved with their peers and in their community. Many people will argue that sports exist only for their own sake and that physical education is in schools only to promote fitness and encourage healthy lifestyles. To be fair, this is certainly an obvious and important aspect of physical education and is taught in many schools worldwide for only this reason. But can fitness be the only reason? If that is true, then why do parents take their children to McDonald's after the game? Surely, if health and fitness were the only beneficial results of physical activity, parents would play a far more active role in promoting it. If parents were that concerned about fitness and health, wouldn't they be jogging laps with their kids and steaming vegetables every night?

—Why Do We Teach Sports?, Sean Slade[19]

I had surveyed over 250 families of children that I was teaching PE to at the time asking them if they wanted their child to play sports as they were growing up and if so, why. Parents responded more than three-to-one that the reason or reasons were mental as opposed to purely physical.

The benefits they mentioned were sportsmanship, the ability to win and lose appropriately, persistence, fair play, teamwork, cooperation, increased personal confidence and self-esteem, enjoyment, socialization, stress reduction, and increased discipline. Parents were more concerned with the development of character in their children than with their physical development.[20]

It was something that Jill Vialet, knew when she founded Playworks, an organization that encourages and helps teach socialization at recess through play. In 1995, Jill was at an Elementary school in Oakland, California, watching an exasperated Principal dealing with fights, disagreements, and disruptions in the playground on a daily basis. Recess had become—rather than a time to relax and be active—a time for frustration and confrontation. Playworks launched as a way to revamp recess into an active, cooperative, and necessary part of the school day. With the students and staff, it establishes rules and guidelines, reinvents spaces that promote activity, reinvents spaces, reduces conflict, and encourages inclusion for everyone in playing. Since their launch they have served over two million kids through more than three thousand partnerships, instilling a love of play.

There is the real possibility that our increasing willingness to overlook the importance of play reflects the larger unhealthy trend of glorifying "busy." For many, the idea that play may be part of the answer to the question of how to build better schools simply doesn't add up when the defining narrative celebrates "doing" almost to the exclusion of "being."

> *But play really does matter. Not just because it contributes to kids' physical and emotional well-being, their academic achievement, and their capacity for trust, self-control and conflict resolution. As play theorist Brian Sutton-Smith wrote, "The opposite of play is not work, the opposite of play is depression."*
>
> *Play is kids' work in that it is a form of experiential learning that contributes directly to a person's ability to handle failure, to work in teams, and to take risks.*
>
> —Nancy Brown, More Than Fun and Games—Play Matters[21]

But what we haven't done yet—or at least not in a system-wide or sector-wide way in this country—is to appreciate and accommodate this need for unstructured play. We have in fact done the opposite. Less free time outside in the neighborhood. Less physical education and even less recess. Even as Playworks has grown, many schools have gone backward. According to the American Association for the Child's Right to Play[22] up to 40 percent of U.S. schools have reduced or eliminated recess since 2000 and those that still have it in place have curtailed what activity can be done during recess. Whether it be fear of injury or lack of supervision we are stunting the individuals' growth by eliminating or restricting a key part of childhood. We may have fewer scrapes and physical injuries, but poor mental health and anxiety continue to climb.

What we are discovering is that we often lose something when we focus too much on an individual aspect, whether that be because we want to increase attention somewhere else or whether we want to ensure safety. We lose more than the activity; we lose key elements that often help make us who we are—individually and collectively—and we don't know we've lost it until it's gone.

Robert Putnam[23] explored similar themes in both his recent books—*Bowling Alone*, written in 2000,[24] which looked at the demise of Bowling Alleys and Clubs and the increase in loneliness; and the 2016 book *Our Kids*.[25]

In *Bowling Alone* Putnam saw the demise of bowling as not just the demise of an industry but as the demise of socialization. In the 1950s and 1960s, alleys, along with other forms of community socialization including clubs, associations, Parent-Teacher Associations, were commonplace and provided a vehicle for both socialization and community building. Bowling was one form of a local, relatively cheap activity that brought people out of their houses and into the community. Bowling alleys were social venues where people could catch up, meet, and grow connections. As alleys were replaced by office buildings, shopping centers, or car parks—structures that brought in more revenue for the same space—we lost something that we didn't realize existed. They were both a place and a reason to socialize. Some gained financial capital and we all lost social capital. In its place remained places to work, places to shop, and places to drink, and often on our own. The bowling alley is an example of this decline in community and socialization that has grown since the 1970s. What we are starting to better understand, or at least appreciate, is the myriad of other benefits we lose when such spaces or avenues to connect disappear.

> *At the outset of our inquiry, I noted that most Americans today feel vaguely and uncomfortably disconnected. It seemed to many as the twentieth century closed, just as it did to the young Walter Lippmann at the century's opening, that "we have changed our environment more quickly than we know how to change ourselves." We tell pollsters that we wish we lived in a more civil, more trustworthy, more collectively caring community. The evidence from our inquiry shows that this longing is not simply nostalgia or "false consciousness." Americans are right that the bonds of our communities have withered, and we are right to fear that this transformation has very real costs. The challenge for us, however, as it was for our predecessors moving from the Gilded Age into the Progressive Era, is not to grieve over social change but, to guide it.*[26]
>
> —Bowling Alone: The Collapse and Revival of American Community, Robert D. Putnam

In *Our Kids*, Putnam extends this social shift discussion to show how the decline of connections and community affects not only our communities but also ourselves. While he draws out the difficulty continuously encountered by those unconnected, to ways out of poverty and the struggle for social mobility, there is another thread embedded in the book that comes via the title. We have moved from a society in which "our kids" used to mean the kids around here, in our neighborhood, to a place where "our kids" literally means my kids only. Our focus has narrowed, and we are, more so, now in competition with our neighbors' kids than we are on the same team. Our circles have become smaller and our goals more precise. And as we myopically focus our attention on this preciseness, we lose what made these connections key in the first place.

> *Caring for kids was once a more widely shared, collective responsibility, but that ethic has faded in recent decades.*[27]

Along with the decline of playing in the street, or socializing at the bowling alley, or joining a community group, we have narrowed our own sense and idea of community. Our communities are becoming smaller, more homogenous, less diverse often to the point where our community becomes our nuclear family.

What do we lose? We lose the broader community and the lessons learned from others' experiences. We lose debate, disagreement, and resolution. We lose the connections, the networks for opportunities, and the supports when things get tough.

> *Before October 29, 1997, John Lambert and Andy Boschama knew each other only through their local bowling league at the Ypsi-Arbor Lanes in Ypsilanti, Michigan. Lambert, a sixty-four-year-olds retired employee of the University of Michigan hospital, had been on a kidney transplant waiting list for three years when Boschma, a thirty-three-year-old accountant, learning casually of Lambert's need and unexpectedly approached him to offer to donate one of his own kidneys.*
>
> *"Andy saw something in me that others didn't," said Lambert. "When we were in hospital Andy said to me, 'John, I really like you and have a lot of respect for you. I wouldn't hesitate to do this all over again,' I got choked up." Boschama returned the feeling: "I obviously felt a kinship [with Lambert]. I cared about him before, but now I'm really rooting for him.": This moving story speaks for itself, but the photograph that accompanied this report in the Ann Arbor News reveals that in addition to their differences in profession and generation, Boschama is white and Lambert is African American. That they bowled together made all the difference. In small ways like this—and in larger ways, too—we Americans need to reconnect with one another. That is the simple argument of this book.*
>
> —Bowling Alone, Robert Putnam[28]

Sports clubs, pick-up games, even just play, have a huge socialization and community-building benefit that we don't truly understand until we no longer have them. Whether it be the bowling club, a community center, the access to fields, courts, or even an open space to play, the benefits go beyond our own personal physical fitness. Via play, whether it be structured or unstructured, we collaborate, cooperate, and communicate. We challenge ourselves, we experience defeat, and we form bonds.

We are connected and interconnected.

NOTES

1. Johnson, C., *Is It Too Late to Bring the Red Fox under Control?* The Conversation, January 5, 2023. Retrieved January 8, 2023, from https://theconversation.com/is-it-too-late-to-bring-the-red-fox-under-control-11299.

2. *ISSG Database: Impact Information for Styela Clava*, n.d. Retrieved January 8, 2023, from http://issg.org/database/species/impact_info.asp?si=951.

3. *Threat Abatement Plan for Predation by the European Red Fox—DCCEEW*, n.d. Retrieved January 8, 2023, from https://www.dcceew.gov.au/sites/default/files/documents/tap-fox-background.pdf.

4. McAnulty, H., *History Talking: Oral History Group Recalls Hare-Raising Experiences*, Central Western Daily, September 14, 2014. Retrieved January 8, 2023, from https://www.centralwesterndaily.com.au/story/2557856/history-talking-oral-history-group-recalls-hare-raising-experiences/?cs=103.

5. Butler, T., *Cane Toads Increasingly a Problem in Australia*, Mongabay Environmental News, April 1, 2005. Retrieved January 8, 2023, from https://news.mongabay.com/2005/04/cane-toads-increasingly-a-problem-in-australia/.

6. Munro O'Brien, J., *It's a Dog of a Way to Get High but Queensland Pooches are Lapping up Hallucinogenic Sweat from Cane Toads*, The Courier Mail, December 16, 2013. Retrieved January 8, 2023, from https://www.couriermail.com.au/news/queensland/its-a-dog-of-a-way-to-get-high-but-queensland-pooches-are-lapping-up-hallucinogenic-sweat-from-cane-toads/news-story/854464b203fcbf60e129dd0c85cbc914.

7. *The Amazon Approaches Its Tipping Point*, The Nature Conservancy, August 20, 2020. Retrieved January 8, 2023, from https://www.nature.org/en-us/what-we-do/our-insights/perspectives/amazon-approaches-tipping-point/.

8. Vu, D., *The "Lungs of Our Planet" Are under Threat*, Discovery, June 22, 2020. Retrieved January 8, 2023, from https://www.discovery.com/nature/the--lungs-of-our-planet--are-under-threat.

9. Viveros, F., & Ladha, A., *The "Lungs of the Earth" Are Really Its Heart: An Indigenous Cure to Save the Amazon*, The Correspondent, July 23, 2020. Retrieved January 8, 2023, from https://thecorrespondent.com/594/the-lungs-of-the-earth-are-really-its-heart-an-indigenous-cure-to-save-the-amazon.

10. Lassman, A., *Flying Rivers of the Amazon Rainforest—A Critical Rain Generator for the Planet*, Pachamama Alliance's Blog, n.d. Retrieved January 8, 2023, from https://blog.pachamama.org/flying-rivers-of-the-amazon-rainforest-a-critical-rain-generator-for-the-planet.

11. Welch, C., *How Amazon Forest Loss Could Affect Water Supplies Far Away*, Environment, May 3, 2021. Retrieved January 8, 2023, from https://www.nationalgeographic.com/environment/article/how-cutting-the-amazon-forest-could-affect-weather.

12. Abrams, R., *Strategies: Entrepreneurs Preventing the Next Katrina*, USA Today, August, 2015. Retrieved January 8, 2023, from https://www.usatoday.com/story/money/columnist/abrams/2015/08/28/strategies-entrepreneurs-preventing-next-katrina/32456567/.

13. Ibid.

14. Simerman, J., *New Orleans' Lower 9th Ward Is Still Reeling from Hurricane Katrina's Damage 15 Years Later*, NOLA.com, August 29, 2020. Retrieved January 8, 2023, from https://www.nola.com/news/katrina/article_a192c350-ea0e-11ea-a863-2bc584f57987.html.

15. Madness, *Our House*, Stiff Records, November 12, 1982.

16. Sahlberg, P., & Doyle, W., *Let the Children Play: For the Learning, Wellbeing, and Life Success of Every Child*, Oxford University Press, 2020, p. xvi.

17. Ibid., p. xiii.

18. Nelson, E., *Building School Community through Physical Activity*, Edutopia, November 19, 2019. Retrieved January 8, 2023, from https://www.edutopia.org/article/building-school-community-through-physical-activity.

19. Slade, S., *Why Do We Teach Sports?* Taylor & Francis, 2019. Retrieved January 8, 2023, from https://www.tandfonline.com/doi/abs/10.1080/07303084.1999.10605884.

20. Ibid.

21. Brown, N., *More Than Fun and Games—Play Matters*, Huffington Post, December 7, 2017. Retrieved January 8, 2023, from https://www.huffpost.com/entry/more-than-fun-and-games-p_b_5997688.

22. Pappas, S., *As Schools Cut Recess, Kids' Learning Will Suffer, Experts Say*, LiveScience, August 14, 2011. Retrieved January 8, 2023, from https://www.livescience.com/15555-schools-cut-recess-learning-suffers.html.

23. Putnam, R. D., n.d. Retrieved January 8, 2023, from http://robertdputnam.com/.

24. Putnam, R., *Bowling Alone. The Collapse and Revival of American Community*, Simon & Schuster, 2000.

25. Putnam, R. D., *Our Kids: The American Dream in Crisis*, Simon & Schuster Paperbacks, 2016.

26. Putnam, R. (2000). Op Cit, p. 402.

27. Putnam, R. D. (2016). Op Cit, p. 226.

28. Putnam, R. (2000). p. 28.

PART II
THE WHOLE OF EDUCATION

Chapter 3

The Whole Approach

Once we understand the need for the bigger picture, the bird's-eye view, we can better focus on both the individual aspects and the bonds that bind them. And if we can't see the bonds, we can assume that they are there. In truth, we have already begun this conversation. We are already taking a step or two back to appreciate the bigger picture and the greater relationships and interconnections between *things*. This is true for our natural world and the impact that we as humans are having on it and many ecosystems.

BACK-TO-BASICS OR FOSTERING SYNERGY?

Education has not been left out of this evolution toward myopia. In fact, one could say that education has been a forerunner in our attempt to narrow our focus on what supposedly *really matters*. The drive to cut expenditure and to—at the same time—raise academic achievement markers has been the promise of many if not most politicians seeking election over the past three decades.

> *Our modern technological society is imposing new demands on schools. . . . Quality education for teachers, recognition of the best in their profession through merit pay, and the restoration of their authority and that of other school officials to maintain respect and discipline in the classroom are essential to guarantee quality education for our Nation's future leaders. We also need to follow a back-to-basics approach emphasizing fundamental scholastic achievement.*
>
> —U.S. president Ronald Reagan, 1984[1]

There were, and are, dissenting voices but we've been having this discussion-slash-argument over "back-to-basics" for several decades now.

> *The people who claim (falsely) that test scores are dropping usually demand more emphasis on basic skills, more traditional instruction, more of the kind of teaching geared to raising test scores. But that's precisely the approach that caused the real problem in the first place—the failure to help kids become thinkers. The more we go "back to basics," the worse things get.*
>
> *Thus, the notion that our schools have strayed from the old-fashioned teaching that used to be successful is dead wrong on two counts. First, old-fashioned methods weren't all that successful in the past either. It may not be easy for us to admit, but those methods caused countless people to give up on school and think of themselves as stupid. Even people who used to be successful students often don't show much depth of understanding, much capacity for critical reflection, or a lifelong love of learning.*
>
> —Alfie Cohen, 1999[2]

We started this book by highlighting the side effects—positive and negative—of medications. But education and educational processes also have unintended side effects. Or rather they have side effects that we know about but, unlike the health industry, we don't feel the need to highlight or expose them.

Yong Zhao, the compelling educational professor, author, and speaker, posed this dilemma in his recent publication *What Works May Hurt: Side Effects in Education*.[3]

> *Medical research is held as a field for education to emulate. Education researchers have been urged to adopt randomized controlled trials, a more "scientific" research method believed to have resulted in the advances in medicine. But a much more important lesson education needs to borrow from medicine has been ignored. That is the study of side effects. Medical research is required to investigate both the intended effects of any medical interventions and their unintended adverse effects, or side effects. In contrast, educational research tends to focus only on proving the effectiveness of practices and policies in pursuit of "what works." It has generally ignored the potential harms that can result from what works.*[4]

With every new drug, and many old drugs, the benefits are weighed up against the harms, and then, only then, is the drug approved or discarded. If the negative outweighs the positive, we dismiss it even if it cures what we first hoped for. There's just too much long-term risk.

But in education, we silo the process and the outcome and fixate on that only. Raises test scores—great! Causes kids to disengage and drop out? Well, that's just an unfortunate side effect that no one could foretell. A way forward would also require a broader view on what we are doing and what we are trying to achieve, and similar to medications assume that all initiatives and interventions have side effects and to expect and debate them.

> *It is extremely rare to find a study that evaluates both the effectiveness and adverse effects of a product, teaching method, or policy in education. I have not yet found an educational product that comes with a warning label carrying information such as "this program works in raising your students' test scores in reading, but may make them hate reading forever."*[5]
>
> —Yong Zhao

What would be the side effects of some educational processes be? Again, taken from Zhao's writing.

- Direct instruction—may raise academic achievement but will likely stifle creativity.[6]
- High-stakes testing—will likely result in increased cheating, exclusion, distortion of instruction, turning teaching into test preparation, curriculum narrowing, and the demoralization of both teachers and students.[7]
- And somewhat counterintuitively, doing well in a subject's testing apparatus can reduce confidence, interest, and self-efficacy in that same subject area.[8]

In recent years, this push and sometimes promise to stick to academics-above-all has also incorporated a narrowing of functions and aims of education—less holistic and more siloed.

There has been a drive to find what will boost test scores without regard for any side effects. And over this period, we have seen the eradication of elements of education that have often been viewed by many educators, students, and families as both worthwhile and necessary.

Since the passing of the No Child Left Behind legislation in 2001, close to half of school districts in the United States have tried numerous ways to focus on the test by reducing recess,[9] nonacademic subjects such as the Arts, Drama, PE, and even resorting to scripted curriculum to "ensure" (inverted commas are deliberate) that students are being taught what will be tested.

And more often than not these reductions and cutbacks have been shouldered primarily by lower socio-economic schools and their communities. Schools that were already struggling with a lack of resources being forced to reduce options and avenues for their students. It has been a myopic push toward short-term gain (test scores) without consideration for what the medium- or long-term outcomes may be (disengagement, lack of learning, dropout).

The soundbites of "reducing recess," "time away from seat time," "being on-task" rings louder in many politicians' ears than the research which shows that in fact these attempts frequently reduce engagement, increase disciplinary issues, and produce no or little gain in test scores.[10]

As a result of this push, and in many cases, requirement imposed via NCLB, to improve test scores in order to avoid school closures, many schools and districts either reduced or severely cut back on a range of subjects that are not directly part of the drive to gauge Annual Yearly Progress. In the first decade of this century, we witnessed cutbacks in Physical Education, the Arts, Music, and Drama. The Center on Education Policy at George Washington University found that 62 percent of school districts had increased the amount of time spent on English language arts or math in elementary schools since 2001, while at the same time 44 percent of school districts were cutting down time dedicated to other subjects.

> *In service to high-stakes "test and punish" threats, schools with the most limited resources have been most likely to cut back on history, art, music and physical education, simply because they aren't covered on standardized tests. Those are the schools where test prep has robbed students of quality one-on-one time with teachers. Teachers have told us that students in their schools have had recess cut back in order to clear more time for test prep, despite abundant research showing that exercise improves learning. Under No Child Left Behind, the testing tail is wagging the dog.*
>
> —No Child Has Failed, Lily Eskelsen García and Otha Thornton[11]

It's like robbing Peter to pay Paul, and then wondering why test scores are still down and student motivation is at an all-time low. The focus then moved from the curriculum being scaled down to subjects being scaled down. If it wasn't going to be tested it wasn't going to be taught.

But this battle is changing. Since the national and some would say global infatuation with high-stake, broad-scale testing and accountability systems focused around academic achievement of the first decade of the twenty-first century, the tide is slowly receding. The passing of the No Child Left Behind Act in 2001 brought greater attention to marginalized communities, but it also brought it via the vehicle of academic accountability and high-stakes testing. In the past two years, especially with the ending of mandatory SATs (Scholastic Aptitude Test) and ACTs (American College Testing) for college entry, the reappraisal of education's purpose and education's worth to society has begun. Not that it wasn't being discussed previously but it wasn't being discussed as broadly as now. Now we have open discussions of the value (or lack of) in some of the institutionalized processes and practices that we have forced our youth to engage in. Do they match and benefit the intended outcomes, or do they actually harm and hinder?

WHOLENESS, INTERCONNECTEDNESS, AND EDUCATION

We have seen a growing backlash to the academics-only, or academics as the main driver, approach in education since the reports of negative side effects of accountability-obsessed schooling that arose out of the No Child Left Behind Act of 2001 (NCLB). Not that the NCLB was intended to be such a driver of high-stakes testing, nor that NCLB was the only example of this movement, but NCLB ushered in a new ethos for education and that ethos was academic high-stakes accountability testing.

Testing has always been a part of education but what NCLB did was to tie it more directly and personally to the ability of an individual school and at times individual teachers to show academic gain in a small range of subjects irrespective of the environment, the resources, or the students themselves.

Schools that could not make and continue Annual Yearly Progress in Language Arts and Math, were warned, had funding cut, and then branded "failing" and forced to close or become a turnaround around with new leadership and new staff.

Motivation of educators decreased along with the interest and engagement of their students. Data became king and the test scores were the only data that mattered. Before too long newspapers were publishing not only every school's results, they were also reporting how individual teachers faired.

Colleagues of Rigoberto Ruelas were alarmed when he failed to show up for work one day in September. They described him as a devoted teacher who tutored students before school, stayed with them after and, on weekends, took students from his South Los Angeles elementary school to the beach.

When his body was found in a ravine in the Angeles National Forest, and the coroner ruled it a suicide, Mr. Ruelas's death became a flash point, drawing the city's largest newspaper into the middle of the debate over reforming the nation's second-largest school district.

When The Los Angeles Times released a database of "value-added analysis" of every teacher in the Los Angeles Unified School District in August, Mr. Ruelas was rated "less effective than average." Colleagues said he became noticeably depressed, and family members have guessed that the rating contributed to his death.

On Monday, a couple hundred people marched to the Los Angeles Times building, where they waved signs and chanted, demanding that the newspaper remove Mr. Ruelas's name from the online database.

—Teacher's Death Exposes Tensions in Los Angeles, Ian Lovett[12]

In that first decade of the twenty-first century, the education of students was decidedly non-twenty-first century. It was by all accounts the height of the test-taking and teaching to that test era. It was didactic, teacher-led, often tracked by scripted curricula that ensured that all teachers were on the same page on the same day, and at the same time. Teachers with less experience, and others more experienced, were provided scripted curriculum to teach page by page, lesson by lesson, word by word. The aim of such curricula was equity in instruction, but it went against everything we know that is successful and effective in pedagogy. Differentiation, personalization, and experiential learning were known and understood methods of pedagogy but rarely got a look in during this era of standardization. In pedagogical terms, it was the dark ages.

And it wasn't just the United States embarking on this journey toward standardization. Other countries soon followed in what was deemed neo-liberal education movement that was based on competition, standardization, school voucher programs, and of course high-stakes testing. The UK introduced its Free Schools—academies that mirrored the Charter Schools movement from the United States. Testing and its accountability repercussions were enhanced and much like in the United States, the test became the driving force in education. Countries like Germany, France, and Belgium soon followed as they jumped on what Pasi Sahlberg, the Finnish education expert, deemed the Global Education Reform Movement. GERM as it was purposely labeled like a virus infecting the educational philosophies and mechanisms from the United States to Europe and into Australia.

One thing that has struck me is how similar education systems are. Curricula are standardized to fit to international student tests; and students around the world study learning materials from global providers. Education reforms in different countries also follow similar patterns. So visible is this common way of improvement that I call it the Global Educational Reform Movement or GERM. It is like an epidemic that spreads and infects education systems through a virus. It travels with pundits, media and politicians. Education systems borrow policies from others and get infected. As a consequence, schools get ill, teachers don't feel well, and kids learn less.

GERM infections have various symptoms. The first symptom is more competition within education systems. Many reformers believe that the quality of education improves when schools compete against one another. In order to compete,

> schools need more autonomy, and with that autonomy comes the demand for accountability. School inspections, standardized testing of students, and evaluating teacher effectiveness are consequences of market-like competition in many school reforms today. Yet when schools compete against one another, they cooperate less.
>
> The second symptom of GERM is increased school choice. It essentially positions parents as consumers empowering them to select schools for their children from several options and thereby promotes market-style competition into the system as schools seek to attract those parents. More than two-thirds of OECD countries have increased school choice opportunities for families with the perceptions that market mechanisms in education would allow equal access to high-quality schooling for all. Increasing numbers of charter schools in the United States, secondary school academies in England, free schools in Sweden and private schools in Australia are examples of expanding school choice policies. Yet according to the OECD, nations pursuing such choice have seen both a decline in academic results and an increase in school segregation.
>
> The third sign of GERM is stronger accountability from schools and related standardized testing of students. Just as in the market place, many believe that holding teachers and schools accountable for students' learning will lead to improved results. Today standardized test scores are the most common way of deciding whether schools are doing a good job. Teacher effectiveness that is measured using standardized tests is a related symptom of GERM. According to the Center for Public Education, standardized testing has increased teaching to the test, narrowed curricula to prioritize reading and mathematics, and distanced teaching from the art of pedagogy to mechanistic instruction.
>
> —Pasi Sahlberg[13]

What has occurred since, and is still occurring, is a discussion on what we have lost by embarking on this narrowing of the curriculum onto core subjects and core content in the pursuit of supposed accountability. Yes, we lost the broad range of content, skills, and subjects being taught, but we also lost an appreciation of the competencies that were not being developed and honed during this time. Teaching to the test does nothing for self-expression or collaboration. It does not build agency nor ownership in study and learning. It is difficult to see how a scripted curriculum could ever spark an interest or a passion for learning in the individual, and it cannot allow for personal preferences or accommodations to learning styles.

By narrowing the curriculum and purpose of education so much we perhaps ironically were able to see how broad and expansive education should be.

Chapter 3

MOVING AWAY FROM THE MYOPIC
AND TOWARD THE WHOLE

The pandemic phenomenon itself may serve to accelerate the solutions as we find silver linings and golden pockets, precisely because of ever-growing dissatisfaction with the status quo, and the new openings that COVID-19 dissolution unveils. The timing is also propitious because we have gained an understanding of so much more in the past five years about learning, technology, people and the most powerful levers for positive transformation. The pandemic has caused us to take two or more steps backwards and, indeed, has exposed fundamental flaws in our learning systems. COVID-19 could turn out to be the catalyst needed to leap forward, but only if we act forcefully on what I call the "right drivers."

—Michael Fullan, The Right Drivers for Whole System Success[14]

In the past decade and especially the past couple of years we have begun to refocus our view of education to see it as more than content and more focused on growing and developing people ready for society. Besides the great work of Michael Fullan, cited above, and his New Pedagogies for Deeper Learning group, we have seen numerous organizations and publications relooking at what education should be about.

- Transforming Education (UN)—education systems need to adapt to the shifting skills needed professionally, making learning more student-centered, connected, dynamic, inclusive, and collaborative, allowing creativity to blossom. Learning resources must evolve to reflect these transformations in how teaching and learning occur.
- Reimagine Education (UNICEF)—a modern education should build and accredit basic skills as well as skills in problem-solving, creativity, critical thinking.
- Education Reimagined—believes a new future of learning is emerging—one that celebrates the wonder, creativity, and endless imagination in every child.
- Education Re-imagined: The Future of Learning—created in collaboration with global visionaries from New Pedagogies for Deep Learning, explores the now, the near, and the next in the changing landscape of education—from traditional to remote to new hybrid learning approaches valuable in your return-to-school planning, and beyond.
- Remake Learning—a network that ignites engaging, relevant, and equitable learning practices in support of young people navigating rapid social and technological change.
- OECD Future of Education and Skills 2030—the Future of Education and Skills 2030 aims to help education systems determine the knowledge, skills, attitudes, and values students need to thrive in and shape their future.

- UNESCO Futures of Education—the initiative aims to rethink education and shape the future. The initiative is catalyzing a global debate on how knowledge, education, and learning need to be reimagined in a world of increasing complexity, uncertainty, and precarity.
- WISE All-IN—a global group that seeks to increase the quantity of *future-fit school leaders* to support schools and systems in their transitions toward resilient and future-thriving learning environments that maximize learner outcomes and well-being for a brighter, more equitable, and inclusive future for our children and our world.

And there is a lot that these groups have in common.

- The drive to see education as the vehicle for societal good and improvement
- A need to expose the "hidden curriculum" of competencies and transformative competencies that are developed during and via learning
- The want to reframe learning as a lifelong endeavor
- A compulsion to place the learner as the agent of change and as a driver in their own learning
- A commitment to engage in discussion about the purpose or purposes of education
- And a desire to see the bigger picture of education beyond the academic.

These groups are actively taking a figurative step back to view the whole of education. They have been asking their constituents, members, and readers to reassess the purpose of education before we launch into the mechanics and processes of education. If education reform merely becomes how do we make this train function more efficiently without first discussing where it's going or why, then we have lost the point of reform. Making the number 4 train to Lexington faster and smoother doesn't do us much good if we decide we want to get to Long Island. Or worse if we never have the conversation about where we want to get to in the first place. In that case, any and all destinations are likely wrong, a waste of time, effort, and money.

The good news is that we in education, much like society in general, are in the process of viewing the whole of education as greater than its parts, and in seeing the process of learning as being as important—if not more so—than the accrual of knowledge. Education in its own way is changing from a noun to a verb. It is less so a thing, a place, a sector, and more so a process and action.

FOCUSING ON THE PURPOSE

So, if education is an action— "a process of doing something, typically to achieve an aim"[15]—then what is that aim? What is that purpose? If the acquisition of content knowledge isn't the core driver of education, then what is?

Before we can truly expand and enhance what we mean by education we must have some agreement on what we are trying to achieve. Purpose—outlined and understood—becomes the overarching driver for education.

Purpose should be intertwined with, and in fact be the most influential force on, education. Purpose should drive education. But for a long time, it has been the aspects—the *things*—of education that have driven it and in doing so restricted its growth and development. These restrictive drivers for the longest time have been the status quo, academics (and a myopic selection of academic content), and the assessment industry.

According to several well-known identities, the purpose goes well beyond the accumulation of facts.

> *What is the purpose of education? This question agitates scholars, teachers, statesmen, every group, in fact, of thoughtful men and women. The conventional answer is the acquisition of knowledge, the reading of books, and the learning of facts. Perhaps because there are so many books and the branches of knowledge in which we can learn facts are so multitudinous today, we begin to hear more frequently that the function of education is to give children a desire to learn and to teach them how to use their minds and where to go to acquire facts when their curiosity is aroused. Even more all-embracing than this is the statement made not long ago, before a group of English headmasters, by the Archbishop of York, that "the true purpose of education is to produce citizens."*
>
> —Eleanor Roosevelt, Good Citizenship: The Purpose of Education, 1930[16]

> *The purpose of education has always been to every one, in essence, the same—to give the young, the things they need in order to develop if an orderly, sequential way into members of society.*
>
> —John Dewey, Individual Psychology and Education, 1934[17]

> *[E]ducation has a two-fold function to perform in the life of man and in society: the one is utility and the other is culture. Education must enable a man to become more efficient, to achieve with increasing facility the legitimate goals of his life.*
>
> —Martin Luther King Jr., The Purpose of Education, 1947[18]

In more recent times the purpose of education has continued to be focused on the potential of the individual and the potential of society.

> *The one continuing purpose of education, since ancient times, has been to bring people to as full a realization as possible of what it is to be a human being.*

Other statements of educational purpose have also been widely accepted: to develop the intellect, to serve social needs, to contribute to the economy, to create an effective work force, to prepare students for a job or career, to promote a particular social or political system. These purposes offered are undesirably limited in scope, and in some instances they conflict with the broad purpose I have indicated; they imply a distorted human existence. The broader humanistic purpose includes all of them, and goes beyond them, for it seeks to encompass all the dimensions of human experience.

—Arthur W. Foshay, The Curriculum Matrix: Transcendence and Mathematics, 1991[19]

And according to one the most influential education voices of recent times—Sir Ken Robinson and his daughter Kate—the core of education can be broken down into four basic purposes.

PERSONAL
Education should enable young people to engage with the world within them as well as the world around them. . . . It is about cultivating the minds and hearts of living people. Engaging them as individuals is at the heart of raising achievement.

CULTURAL
Schools should enable students to understand their own cultures and to respect the diversity of others. There are various definitions of culture, but in this context the most appropriate is "the values and forms of behavior that characterize different social groups."

ECONOMIC
Education should enable students to become economically responsible and independent. This is one of the reasons governments take such a keen interest in education: they know that an educated workforce is essential to creating economic prosperity.

SOCIAL
Education should enable young people to become active and compassionate citizens. We live in densely woven social systems. The benefits we derive from them depend on our working together to sustain them. The empowerment of individuals has to be balanced by practicing the values and responsibilities of collective life, and of democracy in particular.

—Sir Ken Robinson and Kate Robinson, What Is Education For?, 2022[20]

Yet what is both a little ironic and at times depressing the understanding of key voices isn't always reflected in the understandings of the greater public. And today we find via education debates, articles, op-eds, and the ever-present political declarations the public still has a varied understanding of what the purpose of education is. It's almost an argument between the three Rs of reading, 'riting, 'rithemtic, and those of reason, rationale, and readiness for society.

> *Is the primary role of public education to provide rigorous academic instruction? Or is it to promote good citizenship? How about creating a skilled, career-ready workforce? According to the 2016 PDK poll of the Public's Attitudes Toward the Public Schools, there is no clear consensus on the purpose of education. Fewer than half (45%) of the respondents say that academic achievement is the main goal and only one-third of that segment believe that "strongly." Citizenship and preparing students for work were both cited by roughly 25%.*
>
> *When asked to choose, 68% to 21% said they would prefer schools to focus more on career/technical skills-based classes than to offer more honors or advanced academic classes.*
>
> *"The American public does not agree on a single purpose for public education," said Joshua P. Starr, the chief executive officer of PDK International. "And that's despite the emphasis on academic achievement of the past 16 years."*
>
> —What's the Purpose of Education? Public Doesn't Agree on the Answer, Tim Walker[21]

And it has been in this vacuum of common educational purpose that we have launched every possible initiative, project, and program. Every decade we swing—like a pendulum, or sometimes like a wrecking ball—changing our syllabus, curriculum, and schedules based on the prevailing *raison d'etre*, or lack of, often discarding the gains that have been made in the previous ten or so years. We cut subjects and add new ones. Refocus our direction and reword our policies. Update or invent new accountability systems to make sure we are being or appearing judicious. And ironically at the same time, we leave our purpose and mission statements well alone and continuously ignored.

EDUCATIONAL HOARDERS

Status quo refers to keeping on doing what we have done precisely because it is what we have done. Inside this way of thinking is an assumption that value is built over time via use, and while that is not necessarily wrong, it abdicates anything tied to the status quo of true review and evaluation.

This can encompass practices such as class size, subject choice, through to timetabling, and even career promotion. Academic stagnation is the refusal to jettison or even update or change the content that is taught. Content remains king and drives much of the aligned policy and practices for education and much of it—relevant in certain times—has become less relevant in current times. Yet it remains because of our aversion to discard. We have become hoarders of content and curricula, fearful of change and too unsure to confront our real discussion which is what is our and education's purpose.

But much like the hoarder of stuff that crowds the individual's house and makes living difficult, it is the amount of such stuff that makes deciphering the needed from the unnecessary even harder. We are stuck inside the hoarder's house surrounded by well-intentioned stuff but unable to take in the *whole* view. We, like the hoarder who cannot see the house for the stuff, the forest for the trees, cannot see the purpose for the curricula. We have accumulated so much that even deciding to take another look can seem overwhelming. Surely, it's just better to focus on this particular pile and worry about the rest later.

And what drives us to focus on that particular pile—often it's habit, or the syllabus, or the assessment regime. The drivers of our education system have not been pedagogy or purpose for the longest time. Our drivers have been assessments, and standards—tied to the assessments—which have dictated what is taught, why it is taught, and how it is taught. Because if the goal is only to pass a test, then teaching to that test is a logical option. Such drivers, absent from true ethical discussions around purpose, keep us locked in the past even though our current situation requires new ways of looking at issues and new ways of and for learning.

Michael Fullan has written a lot about drivers—both the wrong drivers and more recently about the right drivers. Drivers, as Fullan explained in 2011, "are those policy and strategy levers that have the least and best chance of driving successful reform."[22] A "wrong driver" then is a deliberate policy force that has little chance of achieving the desired result, while a "right driver" is one that ends up achieving better measurable results for students.

The wrong drivers according to Fullan in his 2021 publication *The Right Drivers for Whole System Success*, and who has based much of his career on such declarations, are,

1. Academics Obsession (selfish)
2. Machine Intelligence (careless)
3. Austerity (ruthless)
4. Fragmentation (inertia).

He places these in contrast to the Right Drivers in education and "the things that make us humans . . . [and] by contrast, capture and propel the human spirit."[23]

These are,

1. Wellbeing and Learning (essence)
2. Social Intelligence (limitless)
3. Equality Investments (dignity)
4. Systemness (wholeness).

His right drivers are placed next to the purpose of education while his wrong drivers are the ones that both take us away from any larger purpose and off track in terms of process.

Fragmentation as opposed to Systemness. Inertia versus wholeness. We have focused too much on the *things* of education and not enough on its whole. We have sacrificed cohesion for expediency.

The wrong drivers have been driving education for a long time because we have allowed education to become divorced from its true purpose. Its purpose has been shunned, ignored, or deemed too complicated to discuss earnestly. And in place of this absence of true discussion, we revert to the overarching wrong drivers of status quo and assessment.

Andy Hargreaves and Dennis Shirley outlined this fundamental appreciation of the unwritten or undeclared purpose of education in their book Wellbeing in Schools.

> *Officially, and obviously, the prime purpose of education is not well-being, but learning. Understanding an intriguing idea, learning something new, developing a difficult skill, mastering a challenging concept—this seems to be the essence of education. It's what attracts many teachers into the profession—to switch on light bulbs for children, enable them to grasp or do something they thought was beyond them, help them progress, or introduce them to interests that can turn into lifelong passions.*
>
> *But schools are not only about academic learning. They promote young people's emotional and moral development too. If we act as if learning and achievement are the only things that matter, we fall into the trap of what Dutch professor Gert Biesta calls learnification. Learnification means that anything and everything has to be justified in terms of its impact on learning. Want to secure more time for music in your school? Then point to the evidence that music raises mathematics achievement. Interested in developing meditation and biofeedback among your children? Then demonstrate that the resulting calmness will improve performance on test-taking days. And if you are extending the school day, don't emphasize the value of being with peers, practicing leadership, or*

developing new interests. Just set out the evidence that extended learning time can increase measured achievement.

Alongside learning as we usually understand it, though, schools are also about how children develop. They are about how students experience and express awe, wonder, excitement, compassion, empathy, moral outrage at injustice, courage, playfulness, commitment, self-respect, self-confidence, and many other emotional and moral qualities in their education. Young people need to experience these things not just because of who they will become in the future but also because of who they are now.

—Andy Hargreaves and Dennis Shirley, Wellbeing in Schools[24]

Purpose of education discussions should not and cannot be ignored as they form the basis for any sound reform or improvement effort. They should also not be taken up solely by those in administration or those elected and placed on departmental or ministerial committees. The purpose of education should be a discussion that is engaged in, disputed, and debated by all and anyone involved in education. Which is to say all of us at some stage.

The purpose of education should be what drives our actions in and for education. Not the tests, not the content, not the historical precedence, but the purpose. It should be discussed continuously by teachers and school leaders, by policymakers and parents, and it should be openly discussed—not dictated to—by students.

It is only by understanding the purpose, or perhaps rather purposes, of education from a broad and diverse perspective, that we can focus and target on needed parts of it. We must take a bird's eye view before we plunge from the skies, and then become comfortable in doing it again and again until it becomes habitual.

NOTES

1. *Proclamation 5197—Year of Excellence In Education*, Ronald Reagan, n.d. Retrieved January 8, 2023, from https://www.reaganlibrary.gov/archives/speech/proclamation-5197-year-excellence-education.

2. Kohn, A., *The Trouble with "Back To Basics,"* n.d. Retrieved January 8, 2023, from https://www.alfiekohn.org/teaching/ttwbtbats.htm.

3. Zhao, Y., *What Works May Hurt: Side Effects in Education*, Teachers College Press, 2018.

4. Ibid., p. 3.
5. Ibid., p. 4.
6. Ibid., p. 7.
7. Ibid., p. 14.

8. Ibid.

9. Pappas, S., Op Cit.

10. Reilly, K., *Is Recess Important for Kids? Here's What the Research Says*, Time, October 23, 2017. Retrieved January 8, 2023, from https://time.com/4982061/recess-benefits-research-debate/.

11. García, L. E., & Thornton, O., *"No Child Left Behind" Has Failed*, The Washington Post, February 13, 2015. Retrieved January 8, 2023, from https://www.washingtonpost.com/opinions/no-child-has-failed/2015/02/13/8d619026-b2f8-11e4-827f-93f454140e2b_story.html.

12. Lovett, I., *Teacher's Death Exposes Tensions in Los Angeles*, The New York Times, November 9, 2010. Retrieved January 8, 2023, from https://www.nytimes.com/2010/11/10/education/10teacher.html.

13. Sahlberg, P., *How Germ Is Infecting Schools around the World?*, December 22, 2012. Retrieved January 8, 2023, from https://pasisahlberg.com/text-test/.

14. Fullan, M., *The Right Drivers for Whole System Success*, Centre for Strategic Education, 2021, p. 4.

15. Oxford Learner's Dictionaries. Retrieved January 8, 2023 from https://www.oxfordlearnersdictionaries.com/us/definition/english/action_1.

16. Roosevelt, E., *Good Citizenship: The Purpose of Education*, Pictorial Review, April 1930, archived in Yearbook of the National Society for the Study of Education, October 2008.

17. Dewey, J., *Individual Psychology and Education*, The Philosopher, Volume XII, 1934.

18. King, M. L. Jr., *The Purpose of Education*, Maroon Tiger, January–February 1947.

19. Foshay, A. W., *The Curriculum Matrix: Transcendence and Mathematics*, 1991, https://files.ascd.org/staticfiles/ascd/pdf/journals/ed_update/eu201207_infographic.pdf.

20. Robinson, S. K., *What Is Education For?* Edutopia, March 2, 2022. Retrieved January 8, 2023, from https://www.edutopia.org/article/what-education/.

21. Walker, T., *What's the Purpose of Education? Public Doesn't Agree on the Answer*, NEA, n.d. Retrieved January 8, 2023, from https://www.nea.org/advocating-for-change/new-from-nea/whats-purpose-education-public-doesnt-agree-answer.

22. Fullan, M., *Choosing the Wrong Drivers for Whole System Reform*, CSE Seminar Series Paper 204, Centre for Strategic Education, Melbourne, 2011, p. 3.

23. *Michael Fullan: Author, Speaker, Educational Consultant—Michael Fullan*, n.d. Retrieved January 8, 2023, from https://michaelfullan.ca/wp-content/uploads/2021/03/Fullan-CSE-Leading-Education-Series-01-2021R2-compressed.pdf.

24. Hargreaves, A., & Shirley, D., *Wellbeing in Schools*, ASCD, 2022, p. 31.

Chapter 4

A Whole Education

Education is more than a set of facts and figures to be learned and regurgitated at test time. It is more—or should be—than a system for standardization and conformity. It, as a sector, is a process that is able to raise both our individual and societal potential. But to do so we must understand what is being learned (not taught) and how it is being learned.

Our environment plays a key role in our development and education. Not just services offered by way of the resources available but the climate and culture of the place, the building, or the neighborhood. Similarly, to what was discussed in the section on Our Neighborhoods the school environment plays an oversized role in what we learn and how we learn it. Many schools have taken this to heart and adopted approaches that seek to utilize the power of the environment and establish a culture focused around core themes. This can be both formal and stated or hidden and under the radar—but both are powerful.

HIDDEN CURRICULUM

For the past few decades, we have heard about what has been termed the "hidden curriculum"—what is learned alongside or outside the formal curriculum. It is not stated nor written down, but we know it's there. It is a concept that describes the often unarticulated and unacknowledged *things* that students learn in school—or rather *things* that are learned via school—and that may affect their overall learning experience. The things that when understood and combined result in a more whole-istic educational experience. These are often unspoken and implied lessons unrelated to the academic courses they're taking—*things* learned from simply being in school.

The phrase "hidden curriculum" has been around for a while at least since the 1960s and 1970s in general usage, but it has taken on a new resurgence recently as the formal curriculum has become crowded and overloaded and even the hidden lessons have been pushed aside to make space. It was first used by Philip W. Jackson in his 1968 publication *Life In Classrooms*, which outlined the phrase in 1968. He argued that we need to understand both the celebrated and the unnoticed—the formal and the informal, the apparent and the hidden.

> *School is a place where tests are failed and passed, where amusing things happen, where new insights are stumbled upon, and skills acquired. But it is also a place where people sit, and listen, and wait, and raise their hands, and pass out paper, and stand in line, and sharpen pencils. School is where we encounter both friends and foes, where imagination is unleashed and misunderstanding brought to ground. But it is also a place in which yawns are stifled and recess lines are formed. Both aspects of school life, the celebrated and the unnoticed, are familiar to all of us, but the latter, if only because of its characteristics neglect, seems to deserve more attention than it has received to date from those who are interested in education.*
>
> —Philip Jackson, Life in Classrooms, 1968[1]

After this the phrase was used as the title in a publication by Benson R. Snyder, aptly named *The Hidden Curriculum* (1971). It examined why students, often those who were succeeding in education, dropped out of the education system. The synopsis focused on an area that had rarely been discussed—campus conflict, student anxiety, and personal uncertainty. Snyder went on to shine a light on the academic and social norms prevalent across many institutions and communities, that actually restrict student learning and growth.

> *Socialization is the process by which the new generation learns the knowledge, attitudes, and values that they will need as productive citizens. Although this aim is stated in the formal curriculum, it is mainly achieved through "the hidden curriculum," a subtler, but nonetheless powerful, indoctrination of the norms and values of the wider society. Students learn these values because their behavior at school is regulated until they gradually internalize and accept them. For example, most high school graduates are socialized to either enter college or the workforce after graduation. This is an expectation set forth at the beginning of a student's education.*
>
> —Benson R. Snyder, *The Hidden Curriculum*, 1971[2]

The hidden curriculum has been further explored by Paulo Freire, the educator, and philosopher, and author of *Pedagogy of the Oppressed* (1972), and a leading proponent of *critical pedagogy* and the links between teaching, learning, and social issues. His hidden curriculum focused on the underlying messages and concepts—specifically of oppression and conformity—that a system was delivering via school and its systems.

The more students work at storing the deposits entrusted to them, the less they develop the critical consciousness which would result from their intervention in the world as transformers of that world. The more completely they accept the passive role imposed on them, the more they tend simply to adapt to the world as it is and to the fragmented view of reality deposited in them.

—Paulo Freire, *Pedagogy of the Oppressed*[5]

Freire was presenting the dangers in the inherent norms and regulations that an education system delivers—often hidden inside and via policies, procedures, and processes. Without the space or provision to allow students to be critical and to discuss these norms, they become unaware or unwilling purveyors of these hidden messages and values.

In more recent times *hidden curriculum* has taken on the meaning of hidden skills—often personal, interpersonal, social, and emotional skills—that students learn about themselves and their peers.

Its general understanding has moved from being viewed as an underlying force or influence that seeks to control, to one which highlights the underpinning skills or mindsets that students learn via their school experience. In the current sense, it is viewed far more favorably than it was a few decades ago and refers to the ways the students interact with other students and the things that students learn about themselves. The hidden curriculum very much falls alongside what we may now call or title Social and Emotional Learning (SEL). It is often regarded as the ways we interact with others (social) and the ways we react ourselves (emotional). It encompasses very often the same attributes or competencies that we often list as part of SEL,

- Perseverance
- Resilience
- Collaboration
- Communication
- Experimentation
- Compromise
- Decision-making.

These are *things* that are learned during the process of learning. The things we learn whilst we are learning. These are also often the things that are most respected or revered in a person. The ability to refocus, to try again, to persevere, to rise above. To be an ally, a friend, a collaborator, a team player. To solve problems, think outside the box and persuade others to try a different way.

These skills are also learned and practiced but they are only learned and practiced if the settings allow it. If we actually planned for these skills to be learned and developed, we would set up such opportunities in our lessons or across the day for their practice. Many are doing this already but too often sporadically or in isolation—on islands of educational effectiveness in a sea of standardization.

Varkey Teacher Prize finalist Joe Fatheree in 2016 from Effingham High School, Illinois, and 2017 winner Maggie MacDonnell, from the Ikusik School, Salluit, in the Canadian Artic illustrated their commitment to educating the whole person, drawing out the hidden learnings, purposefully moving away from the constraints of the curriculum, and making them overt.

Joe Fatheree

We spend so much time on learning the science, which I completely value, but we've also got to put equal credit and importance on the art of teaching the maestro the orchestra leader in the classroom who learns how to dance around and to be able to bring the magic out of kids.

I like to tell the story that in kindergarten, if you put a black dot on the wall, they come in and you ask them what is this, they're like that's a polar bear's nose in a snowstorm; it's a fly on the wall; it's a meteor; and they have 9 million different ideas. And the last one is, it's a dot on the wall. And over time something happens in public education, and we get to high school it becomes a dot on the wall. And even at that point, kids are afraid to raise their hand and be able to share. And so we spend an inordinate amount of time at the beginning of the class breaking down the walls that have been built up over time to help kids be able to explore and share their creativity. This is absolutely the antithesis of a standard curriculum.

—Joe Fatheree[4]

Maggie MacDonnell

Whenever I'm working with young people, my goal is to be able to give them the tools that they need to be masters of their own destiny. The definition of a teacher here is a lot more broad than it might be if you were a teacher in Toronto, or Halifax, or Montreal. In an Inuit community, you have this privilege of being able to build very authentic relationships with your students and with the community.

The majority of the challenges that students face are rooted in the colonial history. And as a result, now youth, on a daily basis, face a lot of trauma in the community. Many activists consider that the region of Nunavik to be in a suicide crisis right now. Witnessing the funerals of my students is one of the hardest things I've ever gone through and I never want to be in that position again.

As an educator, I will develop programs that cultivate resilience, hope, and build self-belief, in my students. These tools come together to combat suicidal thoughts. I'm very lucky to be teaching in a project-based classroom so I have a lot of freedom. This year I really focus on a lot on art projects because I find it particularly therapeutic for them to express themselves in those means. I'm trying to create projects for them to contribute in really meaningful ways.

I've always been so passionate about sport and physical activity as a tool to build resilience and young people but I've literally seen it and tasted here on a day-to-day basis. And it's not just about the athletics or this performance these that come along the way there's so much youth development going on when I'm working with my runners. An expression I use a lot is that when you run by yourself you go fast but when you run with others you can go so far.

—Maggie MacDonnell[5]

For both Joe and Maggie, there is more to teaching than the curriculum. There is more than just getting their students to pass a test. For both, it's about inspiring and lighting a flame of curiosity. Joe describes it as the *"art of teaching"* and being able to *"be able to bring the magic out of kids."* Maggie describes it as being able to give them *"the tools that they need to be masters of their own destiny."* And then adds that the role of the teacher is *"more broad than it might be if you were a teacher in Toronto or Halifax or Montreal. In an Inuit community, you have this privilege of being able to build very authentic relationships with your students and with the community."*[6]

Both work across the siloes, the parts or segments of what they formally teach, to bring out what's important and what's needed for that individual and for that class of learners. Both work primarily in that in-between zone aligning what the youth need, to what the curriculum wants. Bringing in relevance, experiences, ideas, and concepts to make them look at themselves and their world differently.

SOCIALLY AND EMOTIONALLY

Social and Emotional Learning is a great example of *things* that should be learned but have been discarded in recent years in the search for better test scores. One of the core *things* that we all need to make us *whole*. But SEL is currently having its day in the sun. The interpersonal skills developed via group interactions, the intrapersonal skills developed via trial, error, perseverance, and the changes that occur in one's self-awareness and efficacy. Hopefully, this will pan out to be more than its *day* and be seen as an integral part of growth, development, and learning but for the moment it is in the spotlight and is being acknowledged for the needed skills and understandings it brings. It's been growing in interest for a number of years and spurred on by the pandemic which, as a result of compelled isolation, has allowed us all to understand the power and value of interactions and relationships.

Recently Nancy Frey, Doug Fisher, and Dominique Smith put out a compelling book titled, *All Learning Is Social and Emotional: The Hidden Curriculum*. It continues this drive toward seeing all of what is taught or rather all of what is learned as being aligned and important.

> *SEL has long existed in the hidden curriculum. This is evidenced any time an adult says, "Boys don't cry" or "Say thank you." Students are learning socially and emotionally all the time, but some of this learning is not productive. If SEL remains part of the hidden curriculum. there will be gaps in students' learning. For example, if students are not directly taught self-regulation strategies, those who have not yet to develop these strategies might be marginalized. Teachers might say that a specific student is off task a lot, or distracted, or can't focus. This is an example of the student being blamed for not mastering something he or she was never taught. When all students have been taught self-regulation, teachers can remind them of the strategies to use.*[7]

They then go on to state the importance of these skills and understanding in life,

> *It's important to stress that social and emotional learning is about much more than developing kids who are nice to one another, cooperative in class, and civically engaged. SEL is also an equity issue. Students who lack the communication and regulation skills needed to navigate a complex societal landscape are vulnerable to becoming victims or perpetrators (and sometimes both). These students are often on the fringes of school and community life, and endure pity, shame, humiliation, and punishment. It is critical for schools to implement systems that develop students' social and emotional skills so that they can carry, practice, and use these throughout their day, at home when the school day is over, and for the rest of their lives.*
>
> —Nancy Frey, Doug Fisher, and Dominique Smith[8]

This focus on SEL, and a more well-rounded approach to teaching and learning, has been growing in recent years. It has moved in some districts and schools, from being an extra consideration to a fundamental base.

Take a look at the key topics and themes for Educational Leadership[9], ASCD's monthly magazine for educators, a leading educational magazine over the past few decades. What we see is a move from themes of assessment, instruction in the early 2000s, to interventions and gaps in 2010. By 2015 the focus is changing toward data, but also diversity and emotions, and by 2020 it is squarely in the realm of social and emotional learning, trauma, and mental health. Certainly, the pandemic has played a large role in this, but we have also seen this train moving along the tracks since the early 2010s.

Why? Well, what appeared before this in the early 2000s? Testing, accountability, and its ramifications from the early 2000s. What was lost in the early 2000s to mid-2010s was the whole. We burrowed down on siloed metrics and accountability systems. We focused on teaching to the test and in separating subjects into concise pieces of data. We shunned recess, the arts, and exercise because they weren't tested or relevant in this data-driven system.

We surgically removed the social and emotional aspects of learning from the process and then found—once removed—that we probably needed them. But the way we have done it is to continue to silo and separate. We have reinserted Social and Emotional Learning often as a subject area, or focus unit as if we should be socially and emotionally aware for only that period or that subject area.

Much like discovering a new organ or section of the body, once we find something worthy of inspection, we dissect it and remove it from the larger body. And then we wonder why that larger body doesn't work as efficiently. We then try to add it back on as an appendage but alas the harm is done as we have cut the synapses that join the body together as a whole.

Yes, a refocus on SEL is important and needed, and our recent pandemic-era teaching-learning experimentation has born this out. But it is the whole of learning that is needed.

Table 4.1 Comparison of key topics and themes for Educational Leadership 2005-2020

2005	2010	2015	2020
Reading Comprehension	The Effective Educator	Co-teaching Making It Work	Mental Health for Educators
Assessment to Promote Learning	Closing Opportunity Gaps	Culturally Diverse Classrooms	The Empowered Student
Learning in the Digital Age	Interventions that Work	Emotionally Healthy Kids	Trauma Sensitive Schools
Turnaround Schools	Meaningful Work	Questioning for Learning	Learning and the Brain
How Schools Improve	Reading to Learn	Improving Schools from Within	A New Reality—Getting Remote Learning Right

Remember those pendulum swings we referred to a little earlier? What we've seen regarding SEL over the past three decades has been a swing against SEL as being superfluous to learning and school in general in the early 2000s. It was a decade where we tried to become more academic, more targeted, and ended up becoming too myopic. We focused on the academic outcomes—raising them and their standardized test scores to a heightened level—with the assumption we were doing the right thing. School was serious. Learning shouldn't be fun. What mattered were numbers and grammar.

In the next decade—along with a correlational decline in, or a societal rise in awareness of, youth mental health and wellbeing—SEL was suddenly seen as the answer. Or at least a bit of an answer. However, rather than raising social and emotional well-being onto the same pedestal as academics, it was crammed into schedules. A little there and little here. One unit as part of Physical Education or Health. Another program for 8th graders before they enter high school. It was the definition of a check-box approach to learning. We tried to get away with the minimum and found—unsurprisingly—that the bare minimum, a token gesture, a sprinkling of skills and understanding, was not enough. It was not enough for our students to learn anything valuable, and it was not enough to refocus our educational obsession away from academics and test scores.

In this third decade of the twenty-first century we've seen the pendulum swing back again but this time it's mainly due to political opportunism and the raising of fear and apprehension. Society and the education community in the United States were moving—swinging—toward a greater focus on social and emotional learning, along with equity and inclusion. The Black Lives Matter movement and the raising in awareness of the discrimination suffered by the majority of the minority populations, including those that identified as LGBTQ, refugees, migrants, has caused a swing back against SEL. And while the pretext for this swing back is primarily political rather than societal, it again has raised the dilemma that there is no true common understanding in the purpose of education.

Those opposing SEL and Equity frequently state that the role of school is academics, and academics only.

> "How much time are we actually talking about [for SEL] as opposed to time for what we think education really should be? You know: reading, writing, arithmetic," Rep. Barbara Ehardt, asked. "When we're talking social-emotional, we're talking about more time spent in an area . . . that really is a role that should be dealt with in the home."[10]

Yet some have gone further claiming that a focus on healthy learning environments or SEL is a trojan horse. Such was the refrain from a parent at a Texas school district during a recent hearing on SEL.

"They use social and emotional learning as a Trojan horse to bring critical race theory and LGBTQ+ curriculum to the classroom," claimed one concerned Texan parent.[11]

The pendulum swings and our demands on education and schools swing in sync. We pick out key aspects, highlight them, discard others, then decide that what was discarded or focused on wasn't quite the right thing. We keep searching for the one thing that will solve/cure/fix education as if we are Charlie searching for the golden ticket in Willy Wonka's Chocolate Factory. That one thing. Is it one extra PE lesson? Perhaps it's a focus on STEM? Maybe if we experiment with Mindfulness? Third-grade reading level? Singapore math? Handwriting! That's it, a return to handwriting!

What makes Charlie and his golden ticket an interesting analogy is that Charlie won because he wasn't obsessed, myopic, or a siloed single identity. He was a well-rounded child who was curious. Some may even describe him as "whole"-some.

THE ABSENCE OF A CORE REASON

If we continue to teach and learn *things* siloed away from others, we continue to see the world as separate or fractured elements, rather than an ecosystem of actions, behaviors, and interactions.

Everything is connected and everything is interconnected.

Teaching subjects in isolation as separate entities does nothing but reinforce this siloed notion. It also robs the subject matter and skills of relevance that they so often need to form meaning and purpose. How many facts or figures or formulae have been learned without a true understanding of their role and purpose? How many students have asked "why do we need to learn this" without getting anywhere close to a sound and sufficient answer? If we can't give an answer to such a simple question, then maybe it's because the reason has long since expired. Or maybe we haven't done a good enough job of aligning its role to the real world and making its relevance obvious.

Math for better or worse often finds itself in this predicament, seeking or being asked to justify its role or roles.

Yes, math has distinct and needed functionary roles in ensuring that we can add, subtract, multiply, divide, buy, sell, save, measure, estimate, and forecast. But math also has a myriad of added or additional benefits that too often remain hidden.

> *A push for students to learn more problem-solving skills will be a central focus of proposed changes to the Australian maths curriculum, with a major review*

expected to reignite wars over how best to turn around declining academic results.

Leading maths and science groups briefed on the proposed changes have called for problem-solving to be central to how maths is taught ahead of the public release of the draft new national curriculum at the end of the month.

In a joint statement titled "why maths must change," the groups said teaching maths content was "no longer enough."

"It is not enough to have knowledge—they must have the skills to take that knowledge and apply it to solve unknown problems, and do it quickly," the statement said.

"The abilities to problem-solve, mathematise, hypothesise, model, are all skills that add worth to acquired knowledge. Mathematics learning cannot sit in silos that focus on content and procedures."

—"Maths Must Change": Experts Push for More Problem-solving in Maths Curriculum[12]

The question too often becomes not how do we *deepen learning* and teach the wholeness of math but rather it gets stuck in the *content versus skills* debate. Is knowing and being able to perform the mathematical equation enough or is it a vehicle through which other skills and competencies are learned? Which is more key to our future success—mathematical expertise or enhanced understanding of our own abilities? It should be both but too often it is viewed as an either-or. Maybe we should be illustrating this *mathematical purpose problem* less with a pie graph reemphasizing the differences lost or gained by the existence of the other, and more as a growth chart where mathematical skills and concepts are learned in conjunction with problem-solving, creativity, and collaboration.

We have begun the wholeness of education already—but only sporadically. Project-based learning takes the skills and concepts being learned and places them into a project—often related to the student's real-world experiences and needs—that needs to be solved. In this way, there are a myriad of skills and concepts that need to be used and improved whether that be math, writing, science, experimentation, teamwork, collaboration, communication, design thinking, etc. Each project, if well designed, has the scope to target skills and concepts that are needed to be learned and each student has the opportunity to design and devise a project that suits their interest and their preference for delivery. It places more agency with the learner, and it incorporates the many skills and concepts being learned into an ongoing activity.

Projects can encompass almost anything as long as they bring in a range of skills, abilities, and content, and aligns to where you want the students' learning to go. PBL Works, an organization dedicated to promoting and advocating for Project-Based Learning and supported by the Buck Institute for Education, highlights outstanding "Gold Standard" examples annually. PBL is described in a little more detail in Part 3 as a way to put a "whole" approach into practice.

Middle school teacher Kimberly Head-Trotter, from Nashville, Tennessee, wanted to continue her students' enthusiasm about the civil rights movement that they had been learning about, and utilize the many historical markers and sites around her city that is more famous for its music scene than its key activist past.

The project she posed to her students was to develop a virtual museum app that would guide people through the rich history of their own city. Students worked on developing the app, March Through Nashville, which brought to life the Nashville sit-ins, school segregation, and nonviolent protests. Stories included firsthand recounts of African American elementary school students walking into a historically white elementary school in 1957 and present-day recollections of the experience, uncertainty, and fear.

Lacrecia Terrance, an 8th grade Science teacher in Louisiana, posed the project to discover why so many local citizens were getting sick with cancer. After collecting research on the entire city, they focused on areas that had the highest percentages of cases and shockingly discovered that the most affected area was where the students themselves lived. Local air quality tests showed that harmful chemicals were being released from the neighboring chemical plants and this along with their newfound agency has pushed them to take more control over their community and its environmental health issues. Students have followed up with proposals to the chemical plants on pollution mitigation efforts that can help their neighbors, their families, and themselves. The outcomes are both tangible in terms of increased awareness and potential changes to local pollution levels, and developmental with the students' agency, confidence, and ability to see the "why" in education heightened.

> *In my experience, I have learned that lower socio-economic students are often disengaged at school, because of many factors such as negative environmental impacts, family and social issues that many of them deal with on a daily basis, wide achievement gaps in their academic skills, having little engagement in lesson strategies, lack of intentional strategies to build self-confidence, and having difficulty adjusting to restrictive classroom environments that do not encourage communication. I recognized the importance of addressing each of these critical components to connect with the students and motivate them to try, so engaging them through PBL was key to my success.*[13]

—Lacrecia Terrance

It provides the context and purpose of the learning. It frames it in a way that aligns subject areas and allows for competencies, skills, and knowledge to be brought in to solve a problem. It de-siloes learning and makes individual subjects appear truncated, and potentially antiquated.

FINLAND AND THE END OF SUBJECTS

Could subjects soon be a thing of the past in Finland? The headline was deliberately designed to cause a stir but are we moving toward a time when subjects are obsolete? Subjects are still taught as inherent stand-alone subjects in Finnish schools, however, they are, and have been adopting a cross curricula and expanded project-based learning approach. They have been taking a step forward in seeking the wholeness of education.

> *In August 2016 it became compulsory for every Finnish school to teach in a more collaborative way; to allow students to choose a topic relevant to them and base subjects around it. Making innovative use of technology and sources outside the school, such as experts and museums, is a key part of it.*
>
> *The aim of this way of teaching—known as project or phenomenon-based learning (PBL)—is to equip children with skills necessary to flourish in the 21st Century, says Kirsti Lonka, a professor of educational psychology at Helsinki University. Among the skills she singles out are critical thinking to identify fake news and avoid cyber-bullying, and the technical ability to install anti-virus software and link up to a printer.*
>
> *"Traditionally, learning has been defined as a list of subject matters and facts you need to acquire—such as arithmetic and grammar—with some decoration, like citizenship, built in around it," Ms. Lonka says.*
>
> *"But when it comes to real life, our brain is not sliced into disciplines in that way; we are thinking in a very holistic way. And when you think about the problems in the world— global crises, migration, the economy, the post-truth era—we really haven't given our children the tools to deal with this inter-cultural world.*
>
> *"I think it is a major mistake if we lead children to believe the world is simple and that if they learn certain facts they are ready to go. So learning to think, learning to understand, these are important skills—and it also makes learning fun, which we think promotes wellbeing."*[14]

The Washington Post took a similar though slightly more nuanced stance. Not quite the end of subjects but the combination of them. Finland wasn't doing away with math teachers but rather seeing how their work and learnings can be combined with other topics.

> Finland's new plan to change school means combining subjects.
>
> In the new system, Finnish schools must give each student at least one unit of instruction combining two or more subjects per year. Teachers are supposed to collaborate with students in planning the interdisciplinary courses.
>
> "We think it's awfully important that when students are involved in the planning process, the topics or phenomena they choose must be interesting to them, so that they are inspired," said Irmeli Halinen, head of curriculum development at the Finnish National Board of Education. "All our work is based on trust, and this trust must also be expressed in schools toward students."
>
> The new approach would be dramatically different for today's students and teachers, but in fact the idea of combining subjects is at least a century old and dates to the American philosopher and educational reformer John Dewey, "who believed that school should be connected to real life," said Larry Cuban, a professor emeritus of education at Stanford University.
>
> "When you teach subjects separate from one another—you teach science, you teach math, you teach reading—that means that there's a divorce between these contents, when in real life, they're not," Cuban added. "When you're cultivating a garden, you've got to know a lot about botany, insects, fertilizer, math, and a whole bunch of other things."
>
> As Finnish educators describe their goals, the program sounds similar to the approaches that U.S. teachers adopted briefly during Dewey's lifetime—before World War II—and again four decades ago, during the years of "open classrooms."[15]

The Finnish Ministry of Education and Culture responded to what has and can be categorized as an oversimplification of the topic and discussion, but also reemphasized the need for students to learn and grow their transversal competencies—the ability and need to work across topics, subject areas and to utilize a range of skills in an ever-growing range of settings.

> The new core curriculum for basic education that will be implemented in school in August 2016 contain some changes which might have given rise to the misunderstanding. In order to meet the challenges of the future, the focus is on transversal (generic) competencies and work across school subjects. Collaborative classroom practices, where pupils may work with several teachers simultaneously during periods of phenomenon-based project studies are emphasised. The pupils should participate each year in at least one such multidisciplinary learning module.
>
> —Finnish Ministry of Education and Culture, Subject teaching in Finnish schools is not being abolished[16]

What we have seen via the evolving Finish system has often been a precursor to what other countries have subsequently adopted. A societal discussion and reframing of education's purpose in the 1970s and 1980s. The focus on equity as a driver, along with the dismantling of standardization in the 1990s. The ongoing and deliberate alignment between health and education as a needed collaboration, and the rise of student choice and agency, school and teacher agency, that coincided with the societal rise in educator respect.

While subjects aren't being eradicated, there is a more concerted effort to focus on the wholeness of learning—how things interact and how what is being learned in one area benefits another area or issue. There has been, and there is, much we can learn and adapt from Finland's education system, but as with all things it must be viewed and understood as a composite and not just individual elements to be replicated.

We are connected, we are interconnected, and the efforts to separate or silo us only tend to harm us. Until we reach that point of realization, and we start the process of putting the pieces back together again, our efforts will likely fail or at best be short-term modifications used for a while until our rational pendulum swings back again.

NOTES

1. Jackson, P., *Life in Classrooms*, New York: Holt, Rinehart and Winston, 1968 (page 4).
2. Snyder, B. R., *The Hidden Curriculum*, Alfred A. Knopf, 1971.
3. Freire, P., *Pedagogy of the Oppressed* (1972), Penguin Classics, 1972, Chapter 2.
4. *Teaching Kids to Stay Creative For Life* | *Joe Fatheree*, United States | Global Teacher Prize. Retrieved January 8, 2023, https://www.youtube.com/watch?v=j2zZCs1uSCw.
5. *The Teacher Solving Problems in a Remote Inuit Community* | *Maggie MacDonnell* | Global Teacher Prize. Retrieved January 8, 2023 https://www.youtube.com/watch?v=mh3gPBmauZg.
6. Ibid.
7. Frey, N., Fisher, D., & Smith, D., *All Learning Is Social and Emotional: The Hidden Curriculum*, ASCD, 2018, p. 7.
8. Ibid., p. 12.
9. ASCD, Educational Leadership Magazine Archives. Retrieved January 8, 2023, from https://www.ascd.org/el/all.
10. Blad, E., *There's Pushback to Social-Emotional Learning. Here's What Happened in One State*, Education Week, June 23, 2022. Retrieved January 8, 2023, from https://www.edweek.org/education/theres-pushback-to-social-emotional-learning-heres-what-happened-in-one-state/2020/02.

11. Alexander, H., *"It's a Trojan Horse for CRT": Now Furious Parents Push Back against Social Emotional Learning (SEL) Being Taught in Schools, Claiming Its Promotion of "Diversity" Is More Evidence of Government Indoctrination*, Daily Mail, November 16, 2021. Retrieved January 8, 2023, from https://www.dailymail.co.uk/news/article-10206207/Youre-actually-advertising-suicide-Parents-push-against-Social-Emotional-Learning-school.html.

12. Visentin, L., *Maths Must Change, Experts Push for More Problem-Solving in Maths Curriculum*, The Sydney Morning Herald, April 11, 2021. Retrieved January 8, 2023, from https://www.smh.com.au/politics/federal/maths-must-change-experts-push-for-more-problem-solving-in-maths-curriculum-20210408-p57hj0.html.

13. *PBL Engaging the Disengaged*, PBLWorks, January 4, 2019. Retrieved January 8, 2023, from https://www.pblworks.org/blog/pbl-engaging-disengaged.

14. Spiller, P., *Could Subjects Soon Be a Thing of the Past in Finland?* BBC News, May 28, 2017. Retrieved January 8, 2023, from https://www.bbc.com/news/world-europe-39889523.

15. Ehrenfreund, M., *Finland's New Plan to Change School Means Combining Subjects*, The Washington Post, November 25, 2021. Retrieved January 8, 2023, from https://www.washingtonpost.com/news/wonk/wp/2015/03/24/finlands-radical-new-plan-to-change-school-means-an-end-to-math-and-history-class/.

16. *Subject Teaching in Finnish Schools Is Not Being Abolished*, The Finnish National Board of Education – Current issues, n.d. Retrieved January 8, 2023, from https://web.archive.org/web/20151226185915/http:/www.oph.fi/english/current_issues/101/0/subject_teaching_in_finnish_schools_is_not_being_abolished.

Chapter 5

From the Whole Child to the Whole Community

In recent years, there has been a growing push to both better understand the role of education and at the same time a desire to better align the sectors and services that focus on education and well-being across the school setting. Now in truth, this push isn't new. We have seen similar approaches from Dewey to Comer, to Kolbe and Allensworth; and we have witnessed pushes to align inside the sectors. What is different nowadays is that the conversation on purpose is constantly with us—buoyed somewhat by our volatile, uncertain, complex, ambiguous VUCA world—and the need for us to be ever more astute in utilizing and focusing on the whole.

IT OFTEN STARTS WITH HEALTH BUT ENDS WITH EDUCATION

The majority of School Health practitioners and leaders have been advocating for a comprehensive or coordinated school health approach since the release of the seminal article by Diane Allensworth and Lloyd Kolbe entitled *The Comprehensive School Health Program: Exploring an Expanded Concept.*[1] This was one of the first times that a comprehensive model was developed that encompassed the whole school and the supports that were needed to aid health. This model, promoted by the U.S. Centers for Disease Control and Prevention (CDC), soon became the preeminent model across the United States and several countries internationally. However, it faced what could be called sector-ism or professional xenophobia by the majority of the education community and was adopted sporadically. What this inadvertently showcased was a widening gap between professionals from different sectors, as each began to hyper-focus on their own parts or areas of expertise. Differing outcomes and measures between health and education meant that rarely the two sectors truly integrated. They coexisted though, often in the same location, which was at least a start.

By the 1990s and into the early 2000s, educators were being directed to focus on academic growth and attainment. Policy was crafted, and accountability measures introduced, that placed repercussions on failure to achieve Annual Yearly Progress (AYP). Most influential across these policy directives was the No Child Left Behind Act of 2001.

No Child Left Behind is based on stronger accountability for results, more freedom for states and communities, proven education methods, and more choices for parents.

Stronger Accountability for Results

Under No Child Left Behind, states are working to close the achievement gap and make sure all students, including those who are disadvantaged, achieve academic proficiency. Annual state and school district report cards inform parents and communities about state and school progress. Schools that do not make progress must provide supplemental services, such as free tutoring or after-school assistance; take corrective actions; and, if still not making adequate yearly progress after five years, make dramatic changes to the way the school is run.

More Freedom for States and Communities

Under No Child Left Behind, states and school districts have unprecedented flexibility in how they use federal education funds. For example, it is possible for most school districts to transfer up to 50 percent of the federal formula grant funds they receive under the Improving Teacher Quality State Grants, Educational Technology, Innovative Programs, and Safe and Drug-Free Schools programs to any one of these programs, or to their Title I program, without separate approval. This allows districts to use funds for their particular needs, such as hiring new teachers, increasing teacher pay, and improving teacher training and professional development.

Proven Education Methods

No Child Left Behind puts emphasis on determining which educational programs and practices have been proven effective through rigorous scientific research. Federal funding is targeted to support these programs and teaching methods that work to improve student learning and achievement. In reading, for example, No Child Left Behind supports scientifically based instruction programs in the early grades under the Reading First program and in preschool under the Early Reading First program.

More Choices for Parents

Parents of children in low-performing schools have new options under No Child Left Behind. In schools that do not meet state standards for at least two consecutive years, parents may transfer their children to a better-performing public school, including a public charter school, within their district. The district must provide transportation, using Title I funds if necessary. Students from low-income families in schools that fail to meet state standards for at least three years are eligible to receive supplemental educational services, including tutoring, after-school services, and summer school. Also, students who attend a persistently dangerous school or are the victim of a violent crime while in their school have the option to attend a safe school within their district.

—U.S. Department of Education[2]

Although it was not the intent of the act, it ushered in a more targeted focus on academic test scores and in particular Math and Language Arts. The NCLB act via its accountability mechanisms became the catalyst for a more blinkered approach to education and a pervasive disregard and abandonment of anything that wasn't directly tied to AYP and keeping schools open.

Subjects, such as Physical Education, Health, and the Arts, were soon being understaffed, underfunded, and increasingly ignored as schools rearranged their curriculum and scheduling. Recess too, as we discussed earlier, became a victim of NCLB as schools sought to maximize the only thing that began to matter—standardized test scores.

The debate over standardized testing grew with the enactment of No Child Left Behind in 2002 and, more recently, with the adoption of Common Core State Standards. Students today take an average of 112 mandated standardized tests between pre-kindergarten and 12th grade, according to an analysis by the Council of the Great City Schools in 2015.

—Katie Reilly, Is Recess Important for Kids? Here's What the Research Says[3]

More testing, more targeting of individual subjects, more attempts to dissect education into what is presumably core. Yet fewer successes.

And while this didn't stop the efforts of the health community to align with education—it certainly didn't help. The health community was increasing its understanding and policy adoption of a *social determinants of health* approach which focuses attention toward the nonmedical factors that influence health outcomes. These are the environmental and social factors that play into and affect our health. It's less so, what viruses are prevalent, and more so, the accessibility to physical activity in your neighborhood. The U.S. Centers for Disease Control and Prevention describes them as "the conditions in which people are born, grow, work, live, and age, and the wider set of forces and systems shaping the conditions of daily life. These forces and systems include economic policies and systems, development agendas, social norms, social policies, racism, climate change, and political systems."

—U.S. Centers for Disease Control and Prevention[4]

In other words, it's a more *whole* view of what causes positive or ill health and how our environments, policies, and processes across the community can have an impact. This obviously includes schools and the education system as they help raise a generation and often set in-process habits which become lifelong and habitual.

So, at a time when education was narrowing its focus, the health community was broadening theirs. And it took almost another decade until the education community began to take the role of health and other student supports more seriously.

WHOLE CHILD

The term Whole Child has become more commonplace in education over the past decade. While the philosophy behind it has been promoted and advocated for decades—Dewey, Maslow, Seligman—if not centuries—Plato, Juvenal—the movement regained prominence in the second decade of the twenty-first century. Whether this was a reaction to the test-driven, accountability-academics above all approach of the early 2000s, the understanding as driven by the health community that environment plays a role in outcomes, or whether this was a realization that the purpose of education was more than content and facts, the movement grew from 2007 through to the current day.

In 2006 ASCD, formerly known as the Association for Supervision and Curriculum Development, a global education association based in the United States, convened a Commission on the Whole Child to, in their words, to recast "the definition of a successful learner from one whose achievement is measured solely by academic tests, to one who is knowledgeable, emotionally and physically healthy, civically inspired, engaged in the arts, prepared for work and economic self-sufficiency, and ready for the world beyond formal schooling."[5]

It began with the posit of the question, "[i]f decisions about education policy and practice started by asking what works for the child, how would resources—time, space, and human—be arrayed to ensure each child's success? If the student were truly at the center of the system, what could we achieve?"[6]

What it sought was a new more expansive, yet deeper understanding of what education could and should be, utilizing the services on offer in the surrounding community and utilizing the potential that education holds. It was a new perspective for education purpose in the prevailing educational landscape.

> *When we commit to educating whole children within the context of whole communities and whole schools, we commit to designing learning environments that weave together the threads that connect not only math, science, the arts, and humanities, but also mind, heart, body, and spirit—connections that tend to be fragmented in our current approach. If the whole child were truly at the center of each educational decision, as ASCD Executive Director Gene Carter posits (see p. 4), we would create learning conditions that enable all children to develop all of their gifts and realize their fullest potential. We would enable children to reconnect to their communities and their own diverse learning resources, and we would deeply engage each child in learning. Finally, if the child were at the center, we would integrate all the ways children come to know the natural world, themselves, and one another, so that they can authentically take their place in creating a better future for all. It is time that the United States begin a new conversation about K–12 education by asking, "What is possible now?" It is our conviction that given what we now know about learning and development, we can do better and we can do more. And when we can do more, then we should do more.*[7]

The Learning Compact also introduced educators to the framework of a Whole Child approach, five tenets that all schools should strive for based on Abraham Maslow's Hierarchy of Needs. Maslow arranged his needs into a hierarchy to illustrate the foundational requirement of one need in order to successfully strive and obtain the next. As he outlined in his seminal publication, "Human needs arrange themselves in hierarchies of pre-potency. That is to say, the appearance of one need usually rests on the prior satisfaction of another, more pre-potent need."[8]

Physiological needs such as food and shelter are more of a fundamental need than Safety. And Safety is more of a fundamental need than Love and Belonging, and Esteem. Yet all are required before one can develop and grow Self-Actualization. One is predisposed upon the formation of the other.

Reflecting Maslow's hierarchy, the Whole Child tenets are arranged in a hierarchy: Healthy, Safe, Engaged, Supported, and Challenged. If the child is not healthy, then how can that child be expected to be engaged or challenged in classroom activities? If the child does not feel physically or emotionally safe, then how can that child truly be expected to think freely, collaborate with others, and explore their boundaries? While one tenet does not need to be perfected before working on the others, there is still an underlying understanding that an imperfect previous tenet will hamper further growth and progress.

Perhaps this swing toward a Whole Child approach was part of the ongoing cycle or pendulum swing of education. What is in vogue one-decade swings out of vogue the next as reform and counter-reform each take their turn at the podium. Or perhaps it was a reappreciation of what many educators now intrinsically—that health, well-being, and engagement, are necessary components of an effective education process rather than expendable extras. Over the past decade, education policy—and to some degree educational philosophy—has moved to incorporate the whole.

It has been increasingly adopted and adapted by various organizations, states, districts, and schools. It has also been adopted and become the mission, direction, or preferred path of many education and health-focused organizations. Over the past fifteen years, the Whole Child movement spread to other organizations starting with the American Association of School Administrators launching their "Total Child" campaign in 2009, to a myriad of leading institutes and organizations including, Action for Healthy Kids; Alliance for a Healthier Generation; American Association of School Librarians; American Association of School Personnel Administrators; American Institute of Research; American Montessori Society; American School Counselor Association; American School Health Association; Americans for the Arts; America's Promise Alliance; Aspen Institute; Association for Middle Level Education; Brookings Institution; Cairn Guidance; Campaign for the Civic Mission of Schools; Center for Civic Education; Center for Mental Health in Schools at UCLA; Center for the Collaborative Classroom; Chan Zuckerberg Foundation; Character Education Partnership; Coalition for Community Schools; Collaborative for Academic, Social, and Emotional Learning (CASEL); Comer School Development Program; Council for Exceptional Children; Directors of Health Promotion and Education; Educational Theatre Association; Engaging Schools; Forum for Education and Democracy; Forum for Youth Investment; GLSEN, the Gay, Lesbian and Straight Education Network; Human Rights Campaign Foundation; Institute for Global Ethics; International Society for Technology in Education (ISTE); John F. Kennedy Center for the Performing Arts; League of American Orchestras; Learning Policy Institute; Lincoln Center Institute; National Alliance of Black School Educators; National Art Education Association; National Association for Gifted Children; National Association for Music Education; National Association of Chronic Disease Directors; National Association of Elementary School Principals; National Association of School Nurses; National Association of School Psychologists; National Association of Secondary School Principals; National Association of State Boards of Education; National Coalition for Academic Service-Learning; National Dance

Education Organization; National Education Association; National Forum to Accelerate Middle-Grades Reform; National Network for Educational Renewal; National Parent Teacher Association; National School Boards Association; National School Climate Center; National Summer Learning Association; Opera America; Phi Delta Kappa International; Playworks; QED Foundation; Responsive Classroom; School Social Work Association of America; School-Based Health Alliance; SHAPE America; Share Our Strength; Society for Public Health Education; Society of State Leaders of Health and Physical Education; SPARK; Special Olympics Project UNIFY; Think Equal; Turnaround for Children; and Whole Education.

Though the place which exemplifies the change in perception, understanding, and adoption of the Whole Child movement can best be highlighted by Governor Kay Ivey's State of the State speech in 2020 where she stated to a room full of conservative politicians and supporters that

> *I am also proud that our Mental Health Department is partnering with the Department of Education to ensure we are promoting "Whole Child." The fact is…our students are with us for at least 8 hours a day and many come from a home life that few of us can imagine. Our students are increasingly dealing with challenges and pressure for which most teachers aren't trained or prepared to deal with; these young people need our help and we are going to do our part.*[9]
>
> —Governor of Alabama, Kay Ivey

Alabama became the most recent state to pass a Whole Child Resolution in 2021.

A Whole Child approach takes two distinct understandings and combines them. The first is that education is more—broader and deeper—than just academics and the accumulation of content knowledge. It encompasses the social, emotional, mental, and physical development of the child as well as the cognitive. Education should prepare the child, the learner, for society.

The second understanding that is embedded within a Whole Child approach is that our health, our well-being, our relationships, our environments, and our support systems, all play a role in our ability to learn and grow. Schools as hubs of education must be key in providing safe, supportive environments which cater to and provide support to individual needs, educationally, socially, and developmentally.

Since 2007 the Whole Child has moved from the periphery of education needs and discussion to being at the table. It may not be core or central to every educational discussion but its core premise that a multitude of factors influence the child's ability to learn and grow and that the growth encompasses more than just academics is certainly central to many policy and funding discussions.

Things have changed and things are changing. As David Griffith, formerly the Senior Director, Government Relations at ASCD, stated,

> It's hard to believe, but when ASCD first introduced its Whole Child call to action in 2007, it was considered controversial. The No Child Left Behind Act was at its height of popularity and influence. Proponents of NCLB suggested that ASCD was backsliding on accountability and becoming an apologist for failure. NCLB's prescriptive and punitive accountability model narrowly focused on state test results to the exclusion of all else. Most damning was that NCLB didn't acknowledge, must less credit, schools that made impressive gains. The system was set up only to penalize schools that failed to make adequate yearly progress. If you're only looking for failure, you're only going to find failure. A change to the incentive structure was needed so that it would both encourage and reward Whole Child educators for going beyond the minimal requirements of test-based accountability.
>
> Complementing the addition of "carrots" to NCLB's "sticks" was the idea inherent in the Whole Child approach that local educators should have more flexibility and autonomy in prioritizing their schools' strategies and plans. A Whole Child education works best when it's customized for the unique circumstances and needs of the community in which the school is located. School leaders are best positioned to create such customization. In other words, educators really do know best.[10]

This whole-istic growth has also become part of the federal government's guidance and direction for education. Terms such as Social and Emotional Learning, equity, inclusion, and well-rounded have been increasingly used in federal education policy and funding over the past decade, culminating in the most recent policy releases and funding in 2022.

> As the nation continues to reemerge from the pandemic, I am proud that the unprecedented resources provided through the American Rescue Plan Act of 2021 are enabling districts, schools, and IHEs to not only recover and rebuild systems and supports to make this vision of an excellent, equitable education for all a reality but also help each student achieve academic success, including closing the gap from pandemic learning loss. Resources from the Elementary and Secondary School Emergency Relief Fund and the Higher Education Emergency Relief Fund are helping schools and colleges invest in the academic, social, emotional, and mental health resources that our students need and mitigate the impacts of the pandemic that, if left unaddressed, would continue longstanding inequities that we, at the Department, seek Miguel A. Cardona, Ed.D. U.S. Secretary of Education to eliminate. Addressing these inequities will help ensure that we meet and exceed the Department's mission to promote student achievement and preparation for global competitiveness by fostering educational excellence and ensuring equal access.
>
> —U.S. Department of Education Fiscal Years 2022–2026 Strategic Plan[11]

This has recently been backed by the passing of a bipartisan bill (HR 1162) in 2022.

Congresswoman Suzanne Bonamici (D-OR), a co-sponsor of the resolution, outlined the need,

> *Students thrive when they have a well-rounded education that includes arts education, physical activity, mental health support, and more... Providing a truly comprehensive education engages students who might struggle otherwise and puts them on a path to long-term success in their personal and professional lives regardless of what path they take. I'm grateful to the village of educators and school support staff who are dedicated to providing children with a quality education, and I will continue doing all I can to support them.*[12]

Similarly, the other cosponsor, Brian Fitzpatrick (R-PA) echoed these requirements.

> *"Our children are our future, and they deserve a well-rounded education that prioritizes not only reading, writing, and mathematics, but also their physical health, mental well-being, and critical thinking skills," said. "The necessity of educating the whole child, especially in the midst of the COVID-19 pandemic, has never been more critical. We must holistically challenge and support our students in their learning environments. I look forward to continuing to pursue bipartisan initiatives that will live up to the goals set by this resolution and ensuring that our children are able to thrive in all aspects of their lives."*[13]

This rise and adoption of a Whole Child approach also fits with the recent appreciation of wellbeing and mental health that the COVID-19 pandemic forced many of us to consider or reconsider as fundamental. During the years 2020 to 2022 (and counting), our need to focus on well-being rose to the fore, and empathy and equity were, at least for a time, key themes and directions.

Disappointingly at the point of writing the US is still engaged in the faux controversy of Critical Race Theory designed by Christopher Rufo, a conservative activist, and boosted by conservative news outlets into another attack on education and educators.[14] And as a consequence, at least for now, terms like "equity," "empathy," "social and emotional learning," and even "whole child" have been receiving a backlash from sections of our community.

The crisis did however, regardless of the current political to-ing and fro-ing of 2022, provide the literal time and space for us to reassess our own set of values. What became clear to many was that health and well-being were fundamental parts of being human and being able to grow and learn.

Whether it was our literal near-death experience or the realization of our need for nature, people, and connections that COVID-19 and its restrictions brought upon us, we are coming out of these years with a new appreciation of who we are and what we need.

Numerous polls have indicated that well-being and health are key to our new mindsets, and we appear to have gone through—or are going through—a cultural zeitgeist and a societal watershed moment.

[A] focus on better self-care, mental health and happiness—LEK insights[15]

[W]ellbeing . . . culture . . . and not being "always on"—PWC[16]

[K]eeping healthy became more important . . . having more appreciation for life and a comparatively lower priority on work life today. . . —Pew Research Center[17]

Slowing down and reflecting on what's truly important has been nice . . . life has slowed down and brought family and friends closer . . . more compassion and empathy and focus on others. —Pew Research Center[18]

School and education – as a mirror of our communities and societies—have not been immune from this shift. Greater focus on trauma, mental health, teacher burnout and stress, and the power of person-to-person relationships, have all been moved to the fore during these recent years. Our schools are more likely now to be seen as places that help the individual grow holistically, tapping into the services across the community, than places focused on the ingestion of content.

There is probably no greater example of this work than that at Tacoma Public Schools, Washington, being led by its Superintendent Dr. Josh Garcia. Adopting a Whole Child approach in 2014, it has been a mainstay of the policies and mission of Tacoma and its communities prior to and during the pandemic. This support and collaborative web has been fundamental in providing assistance, uniting a district, and supporting the health, well-being, and learning of their students, staff, and community members. They have made the school as the physical hub of their communities and placed the whole child as the philosophical heart.

We have been in a storm, relentlessly supporting our students, staffs, and community. Our belief in the whole child, the whole educator, and the whole community has served as our beacon. We may never be the same as we entered this storm. We may not have been perfect, but we know our efforts have been worth it. Throughout this time, we have reminded ourselves and each other that we are truly better together.[19]

—Dr. Josh Garcia

WHOLE SCHOOL

Alongside the Whole Child, and in some regions prior to, there has also been a push for a Whole School approach. This approach "involves addressing the needs of learners, staff, and the wider community, not only within the curriculum but across the whole-school and learning environment. It implies collective and collaborative action in and by a school community to improve student learning, behaviour and wellbeing, and the conditions that support these."

—UNESCO, International Bureau of Education[20]

It sees the school as a system—a wholeness—where learning takes place and similar processes, policies and practices should take place across the whole learning environment. It is an approach to get more continuity across a school and to harness the benefits that come from reinforcing learnings and cross-curricula teaching. Rather than the stereotypical classrooms where the teacher closes the door and does their own thing, it is an attempt to unify and coordinate the strength of the whole environment to help the educational journey.

Such an approach can be focused around themes or directions. These themes can be topic focused such as drama and the arts, or STEM (science, technology, engineering, and math). They can be pedagogically based promoting independence, agency, and self-direction. And they can be targeted to develop our understanding of who we are, and how we interact with the world around us. Several approaches can take all of these, combining progressive pedagogy with core themes and values, and driven by a desire to instill an appreciation of our planet and our role as stewards.

Whole school approaches have been adopted by the Green Schools movement where they "believe that all students deserve the opportunity to be educated in healthy environments that are conducive to learning and support their dreams for a brighter future. That's why we are leading a movement to improve the health, safety, and efficiency of our schools."[21] In these schools, based predominantly in the US spaces and functions such as heating, cooling, and fresh air quality lighting, are used and incorporated across the setting to help develop an understanding of sustainability.

Taken to a further degree, the Green School—aligned but not part of the previously mentioned Green School movement—founded by John & Cynthia Hardy in 2006 seeks to educate for sustainability through community-integrated, entrepreneurial learning, in a natural environment.

The whole school's purpose and processes are framed around a similar core—and in the case of the Green School, it is the core of sustainability. It's a different way of looking and planning the rationale for a school and one that draws in the mechanisms of the surrounding area, the functions of the school, and the input and output of the people to pursue a sustainable future.

As Sal Gordon, Head of School at the Green School Bali explains it,

> *I want to help us all open our minds to a shift in education. I want to help us think outside of the box, I want to help us think of the future. And I want to help us think of them now in simplest terms. I want us to adapt. You know they say change is the only constant, so it goes to reason that if everything is always changing then we continually need to improvise—to bend and to adapt. The ability to adapt is a fundamental life concept and I know I'm not the only person in this room who thinks schools should teach fundamental life concepts so when designing a new paradigm of learning in this ever-changing world. One of the most important things we need to teach our children is the ability to adapt now. The ability to adapt I believe is a fundamental life concept it defines life as we know it.*
>
> —Sal Gordon, head of school[22]

What they do at the Green School is to embed learning into their and the local community. Based on a fundamental set of values including responsibility, empathy, and equality, they integrate with the school community and place the learning into the local context.

This could be as simple as taking learning out of the classroom and having them take roles and duties on the day-to-day running of the school including general cleaning of classrooms, whiteboards, to weeding in the class gardens or taking food scraps out to compost.

They also incorporate service learning into and across the community, tapping into the larger impact each learner wants to leave the community. Their *Footprints project*, for example, is a Grade 5 Capstone and asks students to consider what "footprint" they will leave behind. They express their agency, follow their interest, and see themselves as changemakers.

It is a concerted and deliberate effort to utilize and maximize the mission of the school across the whole school.

Unsurprisingly the majority of schools that take a "whole school" focus also take a "whole child" approach to heart. Both come from an understanding that there is more to the whole than there is in the pieces.

> *We strive to champion a new model of education that nurtures the whole child, giving them agency in their own lives and learning, so that they can thrive with purpose in our ever-changing world. Our "living" curriculum educates for sustainability through community-integrated, entrepreneurial learning, in a natural environment.*[23]
>
> —Green School International, Bali

And for many if not most schools this expands to include parents, families, and the local community.

Themes and topics range broadly, and the Green School is still an outlier in aiming to develop holistic students who see themselves as a core part of the greater world, and as agents, or stewards, of that world. Other topics and purposes are no less key, or needed, and include all ranges of key themes. The common thread being the unifying and collaborative focus on a key theme or direction that spans the whole school. These can include

- mental health and wellbeing[24]
- violence prevention[25]
- trauma[26]
- the arts[27]
- and academic learning.[28]

And sometimes the need for reform and a whole-istic focus on education becomes both a needed frame and an essential set of skills.

Since 1999, Dream a Dream, a leading nonprofit in India, has mainstreamed life skills as a critical approach to help young people overcome adversity while shifting the narratives around the purpose of education to thriving. Dream a Dream, co-founded by Vishal Talreja and led by Suchetha Bhat, brought in a whole child approach to education through the design of life skills programs using intrinsically rich mediums like sports and arts to help young people develop the knowledge, skills, attitudes, and values needed to engage with school and life and maintain healthy relationships with peers, family, and community. Since their inception they have helped over 100,000 young people growing up and dealing with adversity.

As Dream a Dream saw the success of its whole child approach, it also realized that its interventions were still considered on the periphery of learning and were not integral to the experience of school and learning. This led to the introduction of a whole school approach in 2010 by focusing on the school ecosystem and how it can be built around the tenets of equity, inclusion, love, care, respect, dignity, and trust. The teacher became a key lever of transformation in the whole school approach and how each teacher can keep child developmental needs in mind while framing pedagogy, curriculum, assessments, and training. Through listening to young people in their programs, Dream a Dream learnt that they deeply valued a caring, compassionate, nonjudgmental, and trustworthy adult relationship since many a time, they didn't have that at home or in their community. The organization saw, in the teacher, a potential for such an authentic relationship.

This has helped Dream a Dream expand to work with over 40,000 teachers and educators in India and Kenya, helping them unlock their creativity and empathy which has brought fundamental changes in the school environment, in their sense of purpose, and in their relationship with their students. Their Whole School approach was further strengthened in their systems change work with state governments across India. In the last six years, through partnerships with nine states across India, Dream a Dream has introduced several foundational changes to both processes and purpose.

This has included,

- new curricula such as the happiness curriculum, life skills curriculum, value-based curriculums
- incorporating pedagogical approaches that focus and on play, art, project based learning, action-based learning, and empathy-based activities into daily teaching and learning
- designing formative assessments with the focus on life skills, happiness, and well-being
- updating professional development to enhance the whole child and whole school approach.

They have also deliberately planned to walk the talk of whole child and whole school approaches by truly engaging stakeholders into planning and strategy discussions. Their collaboration with state governments comes from a space of listening and co-creating. Engaging government stakeholders as co-owners and co-creators of the whole school approach helped in reshaping power structures and understanding the geo-political context of every region to design relevant curriculum, pedagogy, staff training, and student assessments.

However, as Dream a Dream further peeled the layers of context and nuance in their work with young people in India's complex public education system, they realized that a whole school approach with levers of change around curriculum, pedagogy, assessments, and training still had limited impact. While they were able to develop the life skills needed by young people to thrive and be able to fundamentally change their experience of the teacher and the school, there were larger forces at play that were preventing every young person from thriving in life. Systemic barriers, structural inequities, and sociocultural norms came in the way of helping young people thrive and live up to their potential. This was further exacerbated during the pandemic and the brutal lockdown in India which increased inequities amongst the most marginalized.

Dream a Dream, over the years, has seen many young people take initiative, assume leadership in their community, express fearlessly, ask for support when needed and have the confidence to solve problems and overcome difficult circumstances. *While they continue to build these amazing capacities and agency in young people, they also see the obstacles they face from society-pervasive systemic structures like patriarchy, class and caste bias, marginalization and polarization among others. We know that we have to remove these systemic barriers to ensure that every child has an opportunity to thrive, but it is not easy. As we enter some of these adult spaces while working with the systems around the child, we are beginning to understand how deeply entrenched some of the dominant biases and belief systems are. We see limitations on education opportunities and choices for girls, the invisibility of young people identifying as the third gender, the continued caste and class dynamics that perpetuate inequity, amongst many others. The only place we can start is with ourselves.*

—Vishal Talreja

At Dream a Dream, they are trying to create a safe space that is authentic, diverse, equitable, and inclusive to model a society where dignity of all is upheld. They are starting this whole child and whole school approach by unlayering their own inherent belief systems, stereotypes, and biases as products of this society and an outdated education system, trying to find ways to transform entire societies. They are ultimately viewing their work and their focus to be one that helps to transform our whole world.

WHOLE COMMUNITY

Community Schools—a movement that began in the 1990s in the United States and around the same time as the Comprehensive School Health approach—sought to align schools to their community services, especially regarding health. Though its beginnings were small, the approach was recently awarded $413 million in President Biden's FY22 budget. This amount seeks to help in expanding the capacity of the program to serve up to 2.5 million students, families, and community members in an estimated eight hundred new community schools.

This is quite a leap for the community School movement which has been led for much of the past twenty years by Jane Quinn formerly of the New York-based Children's Aid Society and Marty Blank formerly of the Coalition of Community Schools. Both led the growth during times when community interaction and involvement wasn't seen as essential to learning or development. Originally funded solely by benefactors and grants from the United Way, Charles Stewart Mott Foundation, and the DeWitt Wallace-Reader's Digest Fund, federal and state funding did not come into the calculations until 2010 with the first United States Department of Education Full-Service Community Schools Grant program. This initial grant of ten awards per year of up to $500,000 per year for a school or district, has now in 2022 risen to $68 million.

> *The last two years have taught us how critical schools can be in providing wraparound supports to students and families—such as access to mental health services, basic needs, and high-quality academic instruction. When schools are at the center of our neighborhoods and communities, children, youth, and families benefit. I am thrilled that this program can enable more students and families to access full-service community schools, and that President Biden proposed in his budget to invest hundreds of millions of dollars in community schools, which have been proven to improve student well-being and academic success.*
>
> —U.S. Secretary of Education, Miguel Cardona[29]

Similarly, but separately there has been a push initiated by the U.S. Centers for Disease Control and Prevention (CDC) in collaboration with ASCD, and in recent years adopted by the majority of education and school-health organizations and state departments, to realign the roles and functions of education, health, and the local community to be more synchronized and *whole*. Released in 2014 the Whole School, Whole Community, Whole Child Model, or WSCC for short, provided the frame to better align the supports and services in the school community that aid student growth, development, and learning.

> *Health and well-being have, for too long, been put into silos—separated both logistically and philosophically from education and learning. . . . Health and education affect individuals, society, and the economy and, as such, must work together whenever possible. Schools are a perfect setting for this collaboration. Schools are one of the most efficient systems for reaching children and youth to provide health services and programs, as approximately 95 percent of all U.S. children and youth attend school. At the same time, integrating health services and programs more deeply into the day-to-day life of schools and students represents an untapped tool for raising academic achievement and improving learning. In short, learning and health are interrelated.*
>
> —Whole School, Whole Community, Whole Child: A Collaborative Approach to Learning and Health, 2014[30]

This wasn't the first framework to highlight and align health and education, but it was one of the first to call for a broader whole school and whole community approach. Since its release in 2014, it has become the preeminent school health model in use across the US.

During its development in 2013, and in discussions amongst education and health leaders who were part of the Core and Consultation Group, the case was made to expand the model to incorporate the community. Lloyd Kolbe, the Emeritus Professor from Indiana University, and architect—along with Diane Allensworth, Professor Emeritus from Kent State University—of the original Comprehensive School Health Model (CSH) in 1987, made the case that this new model must be reflective and responsive across the community.

> *Just as the whole school plays its part, the new model outlines how the school, staff, and students are placed within the local community. While the school may be a hub, it remains a focal reflection of its community and requires community input, resources, and collaboration in order to support its students. As with any relationship, this works both ways. Community strengths can boost the role and potential of the school, but areas of need in the community also become reflected in the school, and as such must be addressed.*
>
> *Each child, in each school, in each of our communities deserves to be healthy, safe, engaged, supported, and challenged. That's what a whole child approach to learning, teaching, and community engagement really is about. More than merely a way to boost achievement or academics, the whole child approach views the collaboration between learning and health as fundamental. The development of the whole child is more than the acquisition of knowledge or skills, behavior, or character; it is all of these. The new model calls for a greater collaboration across the community, across the school, and across sectors to meet the needs and reach the potential of each child.*
>
> —Whole School, Whole Community, Whole Child.
> A Collaborative Approach to Learning and Health, 2014[31]

It seems it does take a village—or a whole community—to raise a whole child.

The expansion of a whole child, a whole school, and even a whole community approach frequently starts by expanding the services on offer to learners and often this begins with a focus on nonacademic offerings such as health and well-being.

From the fundamental understanding that the Whole Child Tenets espoused that required a focus on health as a bedrock for development; to the initial forays into Whole School approaches that frequently adopted a well-being thread; to the expansion of community schools and a Whole Community approach which dramatically increased services—especially health—to its students, staff and community members, one has helped lead the other. If one believes that we are more than recipients of facts and that education is there to prepare one for society, then it goes without saying that the learning environment should encompass that. It is not rare nor unexpected that many educators who believe in a Whole Child approach also try to emulate and Whole School and Whole Community focus. In fact, what is rarer are the schools that adopt a community approach but still maintain a narrow focus on academics only. This is a jumbling of philosophies or direction—expansive and unifying on one end and narrow on the other.

When we start to question why something is done, we often start an unraveling of systems. Many of our processes are built of precedent and not on logic—or at least not on logic that stands much scrutiny in our current time. Perhaps we are changing our focus as a society and appreciating that an emphasis on the individual things as individual entities can be as harmful or as useless as not focusing on them at all.

The secret is often in the sauce, not in the individual ingredients but how they mix, blend, and create new and different flavors. Our lives and our systems are no different.

NOTES

1. Allensworth, D., & Kolbe, L., *The Comprehensive School Health Program*, Journal of School Health, Wiley, December 1987. Retrieved January 8, 2023, from https://onlinelibrary.wiley.com/doi/abs/10.1111/j.1746-1561.1987.tb03183.x.

2. U.S. Department of Education (ED), *Four Pillars of NCLB*, Home, December 19, 2005. Retrieved January 8, 2023, from https://www2.ed.gov/nclb/overview/intro/4pillars.html.

3. Reilly, K., *Is Recess Important for Kids? Here's What the Research Says*, Time, October 23, 2017. Retrieved January 8, 2023, from https://time.com/4982061/recess-benefits-research-debate/.

4. U.S. Centers for Disease Control and Prevention, *Social Determinants of Health at CDC*, Centers for Disease Control and Prevention, December 8, 2022. Retrieved January 8, 2023, from https://www.cdc.gov/about/sdoh/index.html.

5. ASCD, *The Learning Compact Redefined: A Call to Action*, 2007. Retrieved January 8, 2023, from https://library.ascd.org/m/21e2f544234c3e97/original/WCC-Learning-Compact.pdf, p. 4.

6. Ibid., p. 2.

7. Ibid., p. 4.

8. Maslow, A. H., *A Theory of Human Motivation*, Psychological Review, 50, 1943. Retrieved December 20, 2023 via http://psychclassics.yorku.ca/Maslow/motivation.htm.

9. Ivey, B. K., *Gov. Kay Ivey's 2020 State of the State Address*, Alabama Political Reporter, February 5, 2020. Retrieved January 8, 2023, from https://www.alreporter.com/2020/02/04/gov-kay-iveys-2020-state-of-the-state-address/.

10. Griffith, D., *ASCD Policy Priorities / Everybody's Talking about the Whole Child*, ASCD, October 1, 2019. Retrieved January 8, 2023, from https://www.ascd.org/el/articles/everybodys-talking-about-the-whole-child.

11. U.S. Department of Education (ED), *Ed Strategic Plans nd Annual Reports*, Home, July 28, 2022. Retrieved January 8, 2023, from https://www2.ed.gov/about/reports/strat/index.html.

12. *Bonamici, Fitzpatrick Introduce Bipartisan Resolution in Support of Whole Child Approach to Education*, Congresswoman Suzanne Bonamici, June 21, 2022. Retrieved January 8, 2023, from https://bonamici.house.gov/media/press-releases/bonamici-fitzpatrick-introduce-bipartisan-resolution-support-whole-child.

13. Ibid.

14. "This entire movement came from nothing," Rufo wrote to me recently, as the conservative campaign against critical race theory consumed Twitter each morning and Fox News each night. But the truth is more specific than that. Really, it came from him via Wallace-Wells, B., *How a Conservative Activist Invented the Conflict over Critical Race Theory*, The New Yorker, June 18, 2021. Retrieved January 8, 2023, from https://www.newyorker.com/news/annals-of-inquiry/how-a-conservative-activist-invented-the-conflict-over-critical-race-theory.

15. Rivlin, A., & Parkin, G., *Consumer Healthcare and Coronavirus: Three Trends That Will Continue to Drive Long-Term Industry Growth*, L.E.K. Consulting, February 16, 2021. Retrieved January 8, 2023, from https://www.lek.com/insights/ei/consumer-healthcare-and-coronavirus-three-trends-will-continue-drive-long-term-industry.

16. PricewaterhouseCoopers, *Redefining Wellbeing in a Post-Pandemic World*. PwC, n.d. Retrieved January 8, 2023, from https://www.pwc.com/mt/en/publications/humanresources/redefining-wellbeing-in-a-post-pandemic-world.html.

17. Sharpe, M., & Spencer, A., *Many Americans Say They Have Shifted Their Priorities around Health and Social Activities During COVID-19*, Pew Research Center, January 5, 2023. Retrieved January 8, 2023, from https://www.pewresearch.org/fact-tank/2022/08/18/many-americans-say-they-have-shifted-their-priorities-around-health-and-social-activities-during-covid-19/.

18. Mitchell, T., *In Their Own Words, Americans Describe the Struggles and Silver Linings of The Covid-19 Pandemic*, Pew Research Center, January 5, 2023. Retrieved January 8, 2023, from https://www.pewresearch.org/2021/03/05/in-their-own-words-americans-describe-the-struggles-and-silver-linings-of-the-covid-19-pandemic/.

19. EdWeek Leaders To Learn From, *Catching Up with Past Leaders to Learn From: Where They Are Now*, EdWeek, February 16, 2022. Retrieved January 8, 2023, from https://www.edweek.org/leaders/leadership/catching-up-with-past-leaders-to-learn-from-where-they-are-now/2022/02.

20. UNESCO, IBE Admin, *Whole School Approach*, International Bureau of Education, May 20, 2016. Retrieved January 8, 2023, from http://www.ibe.unesco.org/en/glossary-curriculum-terminology/w/whole-school-approach.

21. *Whole School Sustainability Framework— Center for Green Schools*, n.d. Retrieved January 8, 2023, from https://centerforgreenschools.org/sites/default/files/resource-files/Whole-School_Sustainability_Framework.pdf.

22. Gordon, S., *Spark Talk—Sal Gordon*. Retrieved January 8, 2023, from https://www.youtube.com/watch?v=4tIbY65FkJU.

23. *Green School International*, HundrED, June 29, 2020. Retrieved January 8, 2023, from https://hundred.org/en/innovations/green-school-international.

24. *Whole-School Approach: Mentally Healthy Schools*, Heads Together Mentally Healthy Schools, n.d. Retrieved January 8, 2023, from https://mentallyhealthyschools.org.uk/whole-school-approach/.

25. Bordoloi, S., & Parkes, J., *Applying a Whole School Approach*, UNGEI, December 9, 2021. Retrieved January 8, 2023, from https://www.ungei.org/blog-post/applying-whole-school-approach.

26. *How We Get There: Whole School Effort*, Trauma Sensitive Schools, January 31, 2019. Retrieved January 8, 2023, from https://traumasensitiveschools.org/trauma-and-learning/how-we-get-there-whole-school-effort/.

27. *Mississippi Whole Schools*, December 12, 2022. Retrieved January 8, 2023, from https://mswholeschools.org/.

28. *Whole-School Model*, CARA, July 2, 2021. Retrieved January 8, 2023, from https://caranyc.org/whole-school-model/.

29. U.S. Department of Education, *U.S. Department Of Education Emphasizes Importance of Full-Service Community Schools Through Competitive Grant Program*, January 11, 2022. Retrieved January 8, 2023, from https://www.ed.gov/news/press-releases/us-department-education-emphasizes-importance-full-service-community-schools-through-competitive-grant-program.

30. ASCD and CDC, *Whole School, Whole Community, Whole Child: A Collaborative Approach to Learning and Health*, 2014, p. 3.

31. Ibid., p. 9.

Chapter 6

Health, Government, and the World

Whole Health, Whole of Government, and even Whole World approaches are now discussed and adopted globally. And while this may appear as different discussions or approaches, they are all embedded in the same generic philosophy that we are more than our parts. That we can gain more in unison. That there is more to us and our systems, services, and solutions that can be achieved by working together in initially collaboration and ultimately in synergy.

WHOLE HEALTH

Health, while a driver in expanding the education system to become broader and more developmental, has also been going through its own metamorphosis with the concept of whole health. There are two understandings key to whole health. One is the commonly understood meaning that our health is interconnected—that an ailment in one part of our body can and does impact our health in another part of our body (or mind). The other meaning of whole health is the understanding that health is connected to our environment and our locality and that our health is a whole of health and a whole of community endeavor. It is not enough that we see the doctor we must also have avenues at our disposal for engaging in activities and actions that are health-affirming—physical activity, nature, human connections, and socialization.

What is one of the greatest determinants of ill physical and mental health in old age? It's not access to a rowing machine, or a treadmill, its personal connections.

In the UK and Australia, the series "Old People's Home for 4-year olds" placed kindergarteners inside a retirement home to gauge interactions but to also track changes in the retirees' behavior, mood, well-being, and health.

> *At the start, elderly participants were measured on cognition, mood, and depression, as well as their physical abilities including balance and ability to get up and walk. These measurements were taken again midway through and at the end of the programme.*
>
> *"We put the older people through a series of well-established tests and some newer ones, but we essentially brought to bear what we know are good ways of assessing the various dimensions of the health condition affecting older people" he explains. The team designed and carried out a six-week programme that gave the two generations time and space to engage physically and socially, including through games, walking, activities using craft and art work and culminating in a schools sports day.*
>
> *And their results were significant. After just three weeks, there were noticeable improvements in residents' measurement scores and by the end of the trial 80 per cent of participants showed improvements. On the sports day, one woman who couldn't remember ever running was seen sprinting off to the winning line with her four-year-old companion. Most significantly, whereas at the start of the experiment nearly all residents identified as depressed, two of them severely, after the six week programme none of them did.*[1]

Improvements that are typically seen in elderly residents as a result of their ongoing interactions with young children include, slowing the rate of cognitive decline, providing a sense of belonging, decreasing the risk of depression, improving physical health, and a stronger immune system. Many also report an overall improvement in their outlook on life. They are happier and more eager for the next day or week with things to look forward to.

And it wasn't just the adults who gained or benefitted. Improvements were also seen in the children with a reported increase in social skills, confidence, and well-being. A study of a similar intergenerational program in the UK found that the children who took part improved their "wellbeing, language use, and acquisition, social interaction, and empathy."[2]

Granted this was not the first time that intergenerational care has been tried—it has been well established in Japan since the 1970s and also adopted in various countries including the Netherlands, Canada, and the United States. But it has placed or re-placed the benefits of intergenerational care back into the spotlight and in doing so reinvigorated the understanding that our health and well-being is as much a reflection of our interactions as it is of our actions (or lack of).

Health is holistic. Health is more than just our individual episodes or aliments—it's a connected web of feelings, moods, interactions, and behaviors. And though we may have known this in our gut for a while we are just starting to act upon it.

As the U.S. Veterans Association (VA) cites, "The Whole Health Initiative is a redesign of health care delivery that focuses on administering personalized veteran health plans rather than focusing on treating disease."[3]

In 2018, the VA launched its Whole Health initiative across 36 VA facilities throughout the country. The project was looking at a way to focus on the wholeness and interconnectedness of health and how an institution such as the VA could utilize this synergy.

> *Providers, clinicians, and leadership are engaged and motivated to implement this new delivery model at their facilities, understanding it changes the focus of their relationships with veterans from one of focusing on problems to one of collaboratively working with veterans to achieve individual health goals. Identified barriers limit implementation and expose issues such as lack of facility resources, hiring and training mechanisms, and leadership endorsement. Whole Health is a priority within the VA and the motivation and readiness of VA staff to move into a more collaborative relationship with the veterans they serve are foundational to the success and longevity of the program. Our findings created an opportunity to promote sustainable outcomes for future Whole Health implementation efforts.*[4]

Adaptations and adoptions of the Whole Health model or frame have sprouted and grown over recent years coinciding with this more holistic way of understanding ourselves and our world.

Recent adoptions have induced the medical sector itself—once bastions of individual diagnoses and ailments.

The Alice L. Walton School of Medicine, in Bentonville, Arkansas, and funded by the Walton (owners of Walmart) family, is currently developing a Whole Health four-year, medical degree-granting program that integrates conventional medicine with holistic principles and self-care practices. It will be one of the first major institutions to take the Whole Health philosophy into medical training and actively focus on mental, emotional, physical, and spiritual health.

> *The School will remain grounded in whole health principles and teaching philosophies, poised to attract the best talent and create a pipeline for a new generation of whole health leaders.*
>
> —Walter Harris, Chief Operating Officer, Alice L. Walton School of Medicine.[5]

The interesting difference here, much like the praise that Governor Kay Ivy of Alabama gave to the Whole Child approach, is that this is a high-profile, conservative family, and company, adopting a more holistic or whole approach. What this shows is that the concepts are moving from alternative, progressive thinking to become more mainstream and commonplace.

The Walton family isn't alone. Cigna, the health insurance company worth $155 billion in 2021, has also begun a more holistic approach to health via its

Whole Health Vision. It comprises six areas of what they call "My World" that make up key parts of our overall health and well-being—Support Network, Home Environment, Work Life, My Family, Financial Health, and Access to Care—and seeks to provide support in each area.

Additionally, they are aiming to have these areas be seen in unison—as a composite of parts—as they state, "these six areas are not separate parts of an individual's life, but part of a whole that are interconnected and affect each other."[6]

Similar to the thematic adoption of other whole-istic approaches, Whole Health has also appeared with respect to causes and issues including domestic violence, substance abuse, through to pregnancy and maternal health.

WHOLE GOVERNMENT

As this holistic or interconnected understanding grows so does its influence over and across systems. Whole Government, or Whole-of-Government (WoG), or even Whole of Government Approaches (WGA), approaches can be seen across numerous governments, national and provincial, and seek to unify approaches utilizing the inherent strength and resources across systems.

It is "an approach that integrates the collaborative efforts of the departments and agencies of a government to achieve unity of effort towards a shared goal," according to the Geneva Centre for Security Sector Governance.[7]

Countries such as Australia, Canada, and the UK—especially under Prime Minister Tony Blair—drove much of the initial focus on WGA in the 1990s. In particular, as it impacted the delivery of services to the public and the benefits of unifying approaches. Other countries, including Finland and the Netherlands, have adopted a whole-of-government approach as a central part of public sector reform. However, it has been Singapore with its small population and centralized government that has embarked on the most consistent use of WGA.

While many countries have and still do take the viewpoint of the service to be delivered (e.g., vaccinations, access to transportation, voting), Singapore has recently moved its focus away from the services perspective and more toward the user perspective.

> *In 2017, the product development team at Singapore's Government Technology Agency (GovTech) was tasked to develop a tool to consolidate citizen-facing services previously delivered by different government agencies onto a single platform. The initiative, Moments of Life, sought to make it easier for citizens to discover and access relevant services during important changes in their lives*

by reducing fragmentation and being more anticipatory in the delivery of those services. Its first effort focused on the very beginning of a citizen's journey, taking the form of a smartphone app focused on making life easier for new parents. The app enabled users to register the births of their children, access their immunization records, navigate healthcare and childcare options eligible for benefits, and apply for the Baby Bonus Scheme (a government program aimed at alleviating the financial costs of parenthood).

Organizing the delivery of services around a citizen's journey, rather than fitting their delivery to existing processes, requires extensive interagency collaboration beyond functional silos.[8]

—Vidhya Ganesan, Yishan Lam, and Diaan-Yi Lin

Singapore, aided by its unique system of government is able to rotate key positions across each portfolio—Culture, Community, and Youth; Defense; Education; Finance; Foreign Law; Manpower; Affairs; Health; Home Affairs; Communications and Information; National Development; Social and Family Development; Sustainability and the Environment; Trade and Industry; Transportation. In doing so they make key leadership roles, and personnel, more aware of the impact of other portfolios, and they can view for themselves the strengths of a more holistic Whole-of-Government approach.

In 2018, Singapore put in place another step toward wholeness in government. They declared that the next focus would move Singapore from a Whole-of-Government approach to a Whole-of-Nation. The difference being the involvement and collaboration with the private sector and nongovernmental agencies.

"A Whole-of-Government approach," according to Singapore political observer Lam Peng Er, "is one that would be state-driven while a Whole-of-Nation approach . . . will be more of a partnership between the Government and different segments of society."[9]

And there is likely no better example of this in action than Singapore's response to the original SARs outbreak in 2003 and the recent COVID-19 pandemic. The government aligned its services and sectors and worked on utilizing their strengths. Systems and policies were created to ensure synergy and require collaboration. Granted Singapore is small and that allows them to do things larger countries cannot, but the national mindset of Singapore is very *whole*.

A whole-government response

Beginning in 2003, Singapore built a task force across multiple government agencies to coordinate interventions and messaging during any future pandemics . . .

During an epidemic, we fight a war against disease, and health care workers are the soldiers. Everyone must rally around their efforts.

As physicians, the two of us directly witnessed the impact of SARS on the health care community in 2003. Health care workers were initially shunned by the public as possible carriers of SARS. But as health care workers became infected, and some died, public sentiment changed and generous donations post-SARS led to the creation of the Courage Fund, which was aimed at providing relief to SARS victims and health care workers.

In the COVID-19 pandemic, the public has rallied around health care workers from the beginning, with an outpouring of gratitude and encouragement.

—Li Yang Hsu and Min-Han Tan[10]

WHOLE WORLD

The communities in which children live today are increasingly more interconnected with the rest of the world. Global economic production and consumption chains, human migration, and the ease of Internet connectivity, and the proliferation of social media have broken down geographic and cultural boundaries. Our local actions—what we purchase or sell, who we vote for, how to get to work—can have ripple effects around the world. Likewise, an action that takes place halfway around the globe can affect our lives. As our world becomes smaller, local communities face challenges such as famine, violent conflicts, climate change, economic inequality, and human rights that threaten the health and safety of children and require complex global solutions. Therefore, an important facet of attending to the health, safety, engagement, and support of a child, and to ensuring that a child is challenged academically, is infusing the mindsets, knowledge, and skills needed to thrive in an interconnected world.

—The Learning Compact Renewed: Whole Child for the Whole World[11]

There is a growing push to see ourselves as part of the greater world. Of course, we are and of course we know this, but we have been operating as if the things we do, and the things that our governments do, do not have an impact beyond our boundaries.

But as climate change, war, refugees, pandemics have shown we are part of this world whether we want to openly admit it or not.

To what extent should our systems, including our education system, adopt a Whole World focus also? It is both the environment we live in—and therefore has distinct influence over our growth and development—but it is also literally fundamental to our and our communities and our society's survival.

The answer should be obvious to all of us that a global focus is not a choice but a necessity.

Many climatologists, city planners, entrepreneurs, and educators, are already taking such an approach. Several examples have been highlighted previously in this book. The work of the Green School Movement and the works of The Green School in Bali in particular exemplify a focus on nurturing our surroundings and developing an appreciation in each child of their role as agents and stewards of our world.

Others could include the work of Greta Thunberg, the Swedish climate activist, or the recent award winners of the Climate Guardians Award such as Wilson Hernan Correa of the project IoT Water in Colombia; and Paula Sapochnik of the Materialoteca project, in Argentina at the recent United Nations Climate Change Conference also known as COP27.

It has also been the work of Luis Alberto Camargo, social entrepreneur, and founder of OpEPA, Organizacion para la Educacion y Proteccion Ambiental, a Colombian nonprofit organization, whose mission it is to reconnect children and youth with the Earth so that they act in an environmentally sustainable manner.

Educational reform should, according to Luis, be framed by a focus on,

- developing empathy, inward (towards oneself) and outward (towards others and nature).
- being open, accessible, and un-siloed.
- collaborative, and inclusive.
- and fundamentally based around a biocentric viewpoint.

Technology and human inventiveness are moving us towards returning to a more sustainable way of life. Nonetheless, changing the way we relate to other living beings (including other humans) is fundamental in enabling us to walk towards environmental peace and sustainable communities.[12]

—Luis Alberto Camargo

He describes this as a shift from being ego-driven to becoming eco-centric, understanding our place in the world and our responsibilities as both agents of change and stewards.

Similarly, Pavel Luksha, founder of Global Education Futures, has our interaction and intersection with our world as a core function of their educational forecasting and planning. Formed in 2008 they have launched innovation projects across the Netherlands, and into the UK, India, Argentina, Algeria, and Georgia, with each maintaining a core belief that education "should be learner-focused, human-centered and nature-informed."[13] It has helped promote and develop a cadre of initiatives' ability to

- adapt and transform,
- embrace future orientations and technological tools,
- to embody well-being of people and planet as our primary purpose.

We have to change the modality in which or economy operates. Cooperate with nature. Instead of taking from it, we learn how to restore it. This opens up tons of opportunities, but also new skills: green skills, well-being skills, etc. [This will lead to] life-centered, transformative, regenerative & circular economies coming to the fore this decade as we move away from "business as usual" extractive capital-centered consumerism. We need to move our technologies from life-destroying to life-saving. [14]

—Pavel Luksha

We began this book with descriptions of the natural and made world and the unintended consequences of our attempts to dissect and individualize parts of it that are fundamentally interconnected to others. The results—some positive but many negative—showcased how we are more than our parts. We are more than pieces that can be interchanged out for another. And because of this interconnectedness what we change in one part of ourselves, or our world, has impact on another, or rather on others plural.

It is somewhat fitting that we end this part of our Whole Systems by focusing on the interplay we have across our world, and begin to question our role and influence as the dominant species on earth.

Interconnectedness implies rather that whether we like it or not all things have influence and ramifications on other things. While a butterfly flap may not cause a hurricane, the premise is the same. At its simplest, the weather influences plant growth, which in turn influences the availability of food and shelter, which influences our health and safety, that in turn influences our ability to travel, trade, and prosper. The converse is also true. And at the same trajectory will inadvertently influence things as remote as our moods, behavior, the rise of diseases, and the likelihood of war and conflict.

We must deliberately move away from a myopic focus on the individualness of things and instead imbue an understanding of our interconnectedness.

NOTES

1. *How "Old People's Home For 4 Year Olds" Might Force a Shake-Up in Social Care*, University of Bath, July 25, 2018. Retrieved January 8, 2023, from

https://www.bath.ac.uk/case-studies/how-old-peoples-home-for-4-year-olds-might-force-a-shake-up-in-social-care/.

2. Tapper, J., *How the Elderly Can Help the Young—And Help Themselves*, The Guardian, January 5, 2019. Retrieved January 8, 2023, from https://www.theguardian.com/society/2019/jan/05/children-eldery-intergenerational-care-advantages.

3. Haun, J., Melillo, C., Cotner, B., McMahon-Grenz, J., & Paykel, J., *Evaluating a Whole Health Approach to Enhance Veteran Care: Exploring the Staff Experience*, Journal of Veterans Studies, May 27, 2021. Retrieved January 8, 2023, from https://journal-veterans-studies.org/article/10.21061/jvs.v7i1.201/.

4. Ibid.

5. *Whole Health School of Medicine to become Alice L. Walton School of Medicine*, Walton School of Medicine, Press release, June 30, 2022. Retrieved January 8, 2023, from https://www.alicewalton.org/whole-health-school-of-medicine-to-become-alice-l-walton-school-of-medicine.

6. *Cigna's Whole Health Vision*, Cigna Global, n.d. Retrieved January 8, 2023, from https://www.cignaglobal.com/blog/whole-health/cignas-whole-health-vision?irclickid=3qOx143I4xyIROCWS30uaQoxUkDRGcyJRUBPyY0&irgwc=1&utm_content=296083_ONLINE_TRACKING_LINK_&utm_campaign=106140&utm_source=123201_adgoal+gmbh&utm_medium=affiliate.

7. International Security Sector Advisory Team (ISSAT), *Whole-Of-Government Approach (WGA)*, International Security Sector Advisory Team (ISSAT), n.d. Retrieved January 8, 2023, from https://issat.dcaf.ch/Learn/Resource-Library/SSR-Glossary/Whole-of-Government-Approach-WGA.

8. Ganesan, V., Lam, Y., & Lin, D., *How Singapore Is Harnessing Design to Transform Government Services*, McKinsey & Company, June 23, 2021. Retrieved January 8, 2023, from https://www.mckinsey.com/industries/public-and-social-sector/our-insights/how-singapore-is-harnessing-design-to-transform-government-services.

9. Auto, H., *Public Service to Go From "Whole-of-Government" To "Whole-of-Nation,"* The Straits Times, May 9, 2018. Retrieved January 8, 2023, from https://www.straitstimes.com/politics/public-service-to-go-from-whole-of-government-to-whole-of-nation.

10. Skerrett, P., *What Singapore Can Teach the U.S. about Responding to Covid-19*, STAT, March 23, 2020. Retrieved January 8, 2023, from https://www.statnews.com/2020/03/23/singapore-teach-united-states-about-covid-19-response/.

11. *The Learning Compact Renewed: Whole Child for the Whole World*, ASCD, 2020. Retrieved January 8, 2023, from http://files.ascd.org/pdfs/programs/Whole-ChildNetwork/2020-whole-child-network-learning-compact-renewed.pdf, p. 27.

12. Camargo, L.A., *Education, What Is It Really?* LinkedIn, August 13, 2018. Retrieved January 8, 2023, from https://www.linkedin.com/pulse/20141028130802-9247365-education-what-is-it-really?trk=public_profile_article_vie.

13. *Global Education Futures*, About Us, n.d. Retrieved March 30, 2023, from https://globaledufutures.org/about_us.

14. *Pavel Luksha on the Future of Skills*, Getting Smart Podcast with Tom Vander Ark, March 31, 2021. Retrieved March 30, 2023, https://www.gettingsmart.com/podcast/pavel-luksha-on-the-future-of-skills/.

PART III

WHOLENESS AND WHAT TO DO

Chapter 7

How It Happens

The question ultimately becomes, even if one agrees with this hypothesis, how much of our learning and being is lost when we dissect our learning and ourselves into pieces?

So, what do we do? How do we transform our education structure to be or to become more cohesive, connected, and whole?

It sounds daunting but many teachers are already doing it. Via Project Based Learning, students focus on a task or problem and then bring in various subject areas, skills, and concepts from across curricula to solve or propose to solve an issue. It brings needed skills and concepts together around a whole problem which has been set as the target or objective to be tackled. It places the issue into its real-world environment, and students get to see how one part aligns to another, creating a building block of learning. In the best cases, the students are unaware of the myriad of subjects, topics, skills used, but they are aware of what they are doing and solving.

PBL, SERVICE LEARNING, AND TAKING THE BROADER VIEW

Project-Based Learning, or PBL by its acronym, is a dynamic and cumulative "classroom approach in which students actively explore real-world problems and challenges and acquire transferable knowledge."[1] It was highlighted in Part 2, Chapter 1. A Whole Education when discussing the need for a core reason.

Its origins go back to fundamental John Dewey principles such as "learning by doing." Part of such an approach places the teacher as the guide for learning as opposed to the instructor of learning. This approach was a precursor to the "guide on the side" (as opposed to the "sage on the stage") philosophy that we have been talking about for at least the past two decades in Western education. In *My Pedagogical Creed* (1897), Dewey outlined his belief that "the teacher is not in the school to impose certain ideas or to form certain habits in the child, but is there as a member of the community to select the influences which shall affect the child and to assist him in properly responding to these."[2]

Learning comes via the process of solving. It is a collaborative process between the learner, or learners, the teacher, and the problem or project. It focuses on learning by doing and learning by experimenting. It requires collaboration, teamwork, and the appropriate social skills and quickly becomes "more than" the acquisition of information and instead becomes learning through the process of learning to solve a problem.

Credit for PBL has also been attributed to the American philosopher Kilpatrick, a successor of Dewey's, as much of his work focused on developing a set of meaningful activities in a social environment that focus on a specific content or on a theme.

Later in the 1960s, Howard Barrows and Robyn Yamblin pioneered the approach in medical training at McMaster University and found it beneficial in process and outcomes. In a 1980s publication, aptly titled *Problem-Based Learning An Approach to Medical Education*, they described it as "a very specific approach to education in medicine, supported by tools designed to facilitate a specific teaching-learning process. . . . Problem-based learning is not simply the presentation of problems to students as a focus for learning or as an example of what has just been learned [rather] it is a rigorous, structured approach to learning that is tailor-made for medical education and based on considerable experience and research."[3]

It soon appeared by many to be tailor-made for traditional education also. The approach was adopted into schools through the 1970s and more formally in the 1980s and 1990s as a way to reengage students and to show how the jigsaw pieces of learning can fit together. A seminal study from Stanford professor Jo Boaler in 2002[4] that compared the academic achievement of students in mathematics over the course of three years found that students who had learned via PBL outperformed students who went to traditional schools.

The key concepts of PBL are not that dissimilar to what we have been discussing in this book. It takes the bigger picture or problem and synthesizes learning from across subject areas and disciplines together to help solve or approach that problem.

According to the PBL Works, a U.S.-based organization dedicated to Project Based Learning, it can be framed by Seven Essential Project Design Elements that will aid the students in students' acquiring key knowledge, understanding, and success skills.

A Challenging Problem or Question

The project is framed by a meaningful problem to be solved or a question to answer, at the appropriate level of challenge.

Sustained Inquiry

Students engage in a rigorous, extended process of posing questions, finding resources, and applying information.

Authenticity

The project involves real-world context, tasks and tools, quality standards, or impact, or the project speaks to personal concerns, interests, and issues in the students' lives.

Student Voice & Choice

Students make some decisions about the project, including how they work and what they create, and express their own ideas in their own voice.

Reflection

Students and teachers reflect on the learning, the effectiveness of their inquiry and project activities, the quality of student work, and obstacles that arise and strategies for overcoming them.

Critique & Revision

Students give, receive, and apply feedback to improve their process and products.

Public Product

Students make their project work public by sharing it with and explaining or presenting it to people beyond the classroom.[5]

—Gold Standard Project Based Learning, PBLWorks

PBL is a trialed, tested, and successful example of how schools and educators are already taking a broader and more holistic approach to learning. It provides both a concrete example of this book's hypothesis and steps for individual teachers to get there.

According to Vanderbilt University, service learning is defined as: "A form of experiential education where learning occurs through a cycle of action and

> *reflection as students seek to achieve real objectives for the community and deeper understanding and skills for themselves."*
>
> *Wikipedia explains service learning as: "An educational approach that combines learning objectives with community service in order to provide a pragmatic, progressive learning experience while meeting societal needs."*
>
> *That second definition is easier to comprehend, but it still feels more complicated than it needs to be. How about this: In service learning, students learn educational standards through tackling real-life problems in their community.*
>
> —Project-Based Learning, Edutopia[6]

Service Learning aligns closely with Project-Based Learning. Both take an issue or problem as the bigger picture and the learning takes place as the students tackle, and potentially solve, the problem. In Service Learning, the problem is a local service or issue. These can include beautifying the neighborhood, helping with underserved populations, advocacy work, through to larger issues such as climate change. One, because there are many, great benefit of Service Learning is that the problem and the services are both real and felt by the local community. The rationale for change is there and the mechanism for service is already in place. The Service Learning process takes students through the stages of Investigation, Preparation, Action, Reflection, Demonstration, and Evaluation, in a meaningful context.

Students are helping with an issue, interacting with those involved, and seeing the effect of their efforts. As a result, it often enhances the empathy and social and emotional development of their students. There is a strong correlation between effective PBL, Service Learning, and effective development of social and emotional learning as much of the practices engages groups, requires collaboration, decision making, consensus building, and thrives on creativity.

Scott Petri, a high school history teacher and the 2021 Outstanding California Social Studies Teacher of the Year, in recounting the value he has witnessed in his students via service-learning describes it as "transformative."

> *Every year,* [my students] *teach me how service-learning can transform students into agents of change, increasing their leadership skills while improving their communities . . .*
>
> *Service-learning projects reinforce SEL because they broaden perspectives, deepen social awareness and connect actions to the needs of communities.*[7]

—Scott Petri

Solving problems and helping the local community take the *whole* big picture and then focus on key parts of that *whole* which are then woven back into the solution.

WHOLE-PART-WHOLE

There is another example where this also occurs regularly and has been for decades. In my early education career, I was a Physical Education teacher teaching not only the skills of sports and activities but also helping develop the learner's self of self, self-efficacy, teamwork, collaboration, and even problem-solving skills. When we taught a new unit or activity, we taught it using the Whole-Part-Whole method. The underlying structure of this process meant that we aimed for the students to experience the larger activity then we would break it down into parts before returning to the whole again.

Whole—try the sport, the activity, the larger project. This allows the learner to experience what we are ultimately striving to learn. It also allows the teacher to gauge the level of the group, ascertain what is needed, and understand what skills or concepts need to be focused on first.

Part—focus on one or two key parts of the sport or activity that are fundamental in improving. This may be a skill around passing or shooting; it may be a concept around positional lay and moving; it may be a drill that directs attention toward a combination of skills together.

Whole—return the game or activity to test and trial the newfound skills and concepts. This is where you return to use the skills in the real world—the real world in this case being the game.

Whole Versus Part Practice

The whole method of practice is obvious: The whole technique is practiced intact. The part method is actually the whole-part-whole method. You teach the whole method as just outlined, practice it in parts, and then recombine the parts back into the whole via practice.

What's the best method to use? When possible, it's best to practice the whole technique; this avoids spending time combining the parts back into the whole and helps your athletes learn how to use the technique in the context of a contest. However, if the technique is so complex that athletes can't develop a good mental plan (the first stage of learning), then you should break the technique into parts.

When to Break Techniques into Parts

To decide whether to break a technical skill into parts, you need to evaluate the task on two dimensions: its complexity and the interdependence of the parts.

Two questions will help you determine task complexity, or how difficult it may be for athletes to develop a good mental plan:
   How many parts are there to the task?
   How mentally demanding is the task?
   Next, you need to evaluate how interdependent or independent the parts of the task are. That is, how closely is one part of the technique related to the next? For example, in the tennis serve, you can fairly easily separate the ball toss from the swing of the racket, but you really can't separate the racket swing and contact with the ball from the follow-through.

—Rainer Martens[8]

And such an approach doesn't only apply to skill development—it can also be applied to anything being learned via the game, activity or sport including Game Sense. The Game Sense teaching and coaching approach is a game-based and player-centered sport teaching pedagogy that champions the development of "thinking players." According to Shane Pill, an Australian Associate Professor, at the School of Education at Flinders University, and proponent of Game Sense, it exists in three parts:

- Decision Making—knowing what to do in the context of play.
- Movement Knowledge—knowing how to do it.
- Movement Capability—the ability to execute the response successfully.

Game Sense is understanding how the game is played and has, however, also been used as a synonym for tactical game intelligence and the "thinking" player (i.e. player game sense) (Charlesworth, 1993; Launder, 2001). Game Sense approach is distinguished from other game-centred approaches providing the opportunity to learn through play. It does not incorporate the step-by-step game appreciation-to-performance model "fundamental" (Bunker & Thorpe, 1986, p.7) and "critical" (Waring & Almond, 1995) to the teaching games for understanding (TGfU) models. The separation of tactical before technical, or progress from tactics to skills (Hopper, 2002; Waring & Almond, 1995) is not emphasised in Game Sense coaching literature. The Game Sense approach is analogous to whole-part-whole (Reid, 2003) rather than the step-by-step tactical model description (Metzler, 2011). The Game Sense approach suggests individual player technical movement models, game understanding and tactical decision making are not separate skills but interrelated (Pill, 2013c). The Game Sense approach is considered more flexible (Light, 2013) and yet in some ways more sophisticated (Kidman, 2001) than other game-centred approaches.

—Shane Pill[9]

Whole-Part-Part is an approach that can work across multiple areas or settings. It takes a larger picture and plays it out, then focuses on areas of need, before returning to the larger picture.

What it does require, however, is a concerted discussion and common understanding on what the larger picture is or should be. And to a certain extent, this is where we began this education section of the book, with a discussion on educational purpose. Because without that discussion the remaining and subsequent debates and strategies become irrelevant.

What do we want, what do we need, our children to learn and become? We as individuals and we as a community and society. This seems an obvious question but is too often ignored or bypassed as we scramble to pass new educational policy.

COMMONALITY OF OBJECTIVE AND MINDSET

Whether it is a humanistic Physical Education class or a Service Learning project run via the local community, the commonalities that need to exist are twofold.

Objectives and mindsets.

First, there needs to be commonality on what the objective of the learning is. This sounds logical but too often we jump over, dismiss, or deliberately ignore this question.

In my 2022 book *Questioning Education: Moving from What and How to Why and Who,* I outlined this fundamental step (and flaw) in our planning of effective learning systems.

> *Why have we not been able to prise away this discussion on the purpose of education from the philosophers to the practitioners? Why have we not been able to empower the learners and the teachers themselves in this necessary dialogue? We have left the discussion of purpose to those who have succeeded out of a system that has benefited them but alienated others. We should be raising the fundamental questions of purpose with and across those who are not fitting in with the current system as much as we do with those for whom it has been constructed.*
>
> *And my premise—and it is just a premise—is that we have been asking the wrong questions of education's purpose from the start. Or at least the purpose of education needs to change from teaching us what we should know to why we should know it.*[10]

—Sean Slade

We have had debates over content—the Sciences versus the Arts, Language Arts versus Algebra, European History versus African-American Studies. We've had debates over the teaching styles—Singapore Math, Direct Instruction, Peer to Peer learning. We've even had debates over texting, handwriting, and cursive. But what we haven't truly had is a debate about the purpose of education. And consequently, the purpose of what a teacher is trying to teach and the student learn.

Is it just the acquisition of content and skills? Is it just to get a job, and have a career? Or is it more so to develop the potential of the (whole) individual, as they enter society? Is it also about growing and developing the (whole) community, and being active participants in who we want (as a whole) to become?

These discussions are foundational in our understanding of where we intend to go. They are needed and a prerequisite at the broader, bigger picture level, so that we can have them also at the local or school level. If we were setting out on a journey, we would have a destination in mind. It could be a physical destination or even a philosophical one. It may be Paris or it may be "to discover more about the world" or to "learn about how other people live," or even to "find out more about myself." We may end up going to the same physical location, such as Paris, but we may be there for varying reasons and seeking different outcomes. What we then do and see there is dependent upon what we are seeking.

It is the same with education. We must understand what our destination or objective(s) is. What occurs in the learning (what we do in Paris to continue the analogy) depends upon it. If we don't have that discussion we all head to Paris—or worse somewhere that we haven't truly decided should be a destination—without a clear rationale for why we are there and what we are looking for. We all end up heading to Paris or to Washington DC or to London simply because that's what we've always done. But we don't really know why we're there.

Until we have these larger purpose and destination debates, we will likely be stuck in the quagmire of the same old educational debates we've been having for the past quarter century. Debates that we take seriously and with a fair dose of passion, but debates that are separated from the larger purpose. Maybe we won't go back to arguing over the number of seat time minutes, or whether taking a recess break is good for pedagogy, or whether schools should begin before 7:30 a.m., but we have an opportunity here and now to take a step toward having a serious discussion about our purpose in and for education.

If there was ever a sector, or an industry, that should be at the cutting edge of innovation, it is education, whose whole raison d'etre is preparing those soon to be living in the future for the future. Yet education for too long has appeared less the sails of a ship pushing it forward to new horizons and more of the anchor stuck to a sea floor and restricting its own progress. 2020 and 2021, it seems, has compelled us to raise the anchor from the rocks and we are starting to discuss where we want to go. Sure, the spinnaker hasn't yet been cast but the crew are at least talking.[11]

—Sean Slade

The second commonality we need in order to move forward is simpler but probably just as impactful. We need commonality of mindset. We need educators to see the whole of learning. For them to understand that they are both teaching from a holistic perspective—the whole child—and also that they are part of the whole of learning. They along with the other teachers, the community, the students, their families, and society at large, are all helping the child learn, grow, and develop. We are in this together.

And these two commonalities—the purpose of education and the whole mindset—are also connected and interconnected.

We have had a closed mindset of *individualism* promoted in education for many decades. It's both in *individualism* of teaching—close the door, teach your material, wait for the bell, do it again. How does what you're teaching fit within the broader context? Doesn't matter, that's for someone else to decide—I just do my own thing and do it well.

And it's also in *individualism* in learning—individual subjects, individual scores, and individual growth. These things aren't necessarily wrong, but they do support and propagate the other each other. If the teaching is based on an individual approach, delivered in individual lessons, by individual teachers, then the learning will automatically follow. The closing of the classroom door just re-emphasizes this. Together they promote a siloed, individual focus on and about education. They perpetuate the notion that education is a set of individual things, delivered by individual people, in individual lessons.

Our behaviors stem from our mindsets. But our mindsets are also influenced by our behaviors and actions. Similar to a self-fulfilling prophecy, what we do reinforces what we believe and what we believe influences what we do. If you believe that grading students on a bell curve is fundamental and you are supported in this belief by the system and leadership, then you continue to do it as you are being supported and rewarded. Your goals become more finite and discreet and your teaching more targeted toward that goal. You close the door—figuratively and possibly literally—to seeing how others teach and you focus on your classes and your outcomes. Your goals aren't encumbered by the bigger picture of purpose they are precise and measurable. They are guided by a mindset of compliance and individualism without having embarked on the larger question of why.

Yet if we are able to change the mindsets of educators, and society as a whole (there's that word again), that there is more to the whole than there is in the parts. That education is more than academics and the acquisition of content and skills, but rather is preparing our youth for life.

That we each play a role in the education journey.

And our mindsets can be influenced by our actions. The longer we go without discussing the bigger picture the more we find ourselves caught up debates that, while important, are not key. We become contently frustrated in our own world.

The more we discuss the bigger picture and rationale for education, the more we see this as fundamental to what we do.

Mindsets influence behavior which in turn impacts our actions. These actions then support our mindsets. It becomes a virtuous or vicious cycle. It becomes a self-fulfilling prophecy.

NOTES

1. *Project-Based Learning (PBL)*, Edutopia, https://www.edutopia.org/project-based-learning.

2. Dewey, J., *My Pedagogic Creed*, School Journal, 54(3), 77–80, 1897.

3. Barrows, H. S., & Tamblyn, R. M., *Problem-based learning: An Approach to Medical Education*, Springer Publishing Company, 1980. Retrieved March 18, 2023, from https://app.nova.edu/toolbox/instructionalproducts/edd8124/fall11/1980-BarrowsTamblyn-PBL.pdf.

4. Boaler, J., *Learning from Teaching*: *Exploring the Relationship between Reform Curriculum and Equity*, Journal for Research in Mathematics Education, 33(4), 239–58, 2002.

5. *Gold Standard Project Based Learning*, PBLWorks, n.d. Retrieved March 18, 2023, https://www.pblworks.org/what-is-pbl/gold-standard-project-design.

6. *Service Learning*, Edutopia, n.d. Retrieved March 18, 2023, https://www.edutopia.org/blog/what-heck-service-learning-heather-wolpert-gawron.

7. Petri, S., *Service-Learning Can Be the Bridge to Social Emotional Learning. Educators Should Embrace It*, EdSurge, September 6, 2022. Retrieved March 16, 2023, from https://www.edsurge.com/news/2022-09-06-service-learning-can-be-the-bridge-to-social-emotional-learning-educators-should-embrace-it.

8. Martens, R., *Successful Coaching, 4th Edition*, The Games Approach, Human Kinetics, 2012, Chapter 9.

9. Pill, S., *Coach Development through Collaborative Action Research: An Australian Football Coach's Implementation of a Game Sense Approach*, University of Sydney Papers in HMHCE—Special Games Sense Edition 2014, p. 35.

10. Slade, S., *Questioning Education: Moving from What & How to Why & Who*, Routledge, 2022, p. 1.

11. Ibid., p. 2.

Chapter 8

A Collaborative, Collective Focus

There has been a swing toward a more holistic approach to leadership, and educational leadership specifically, over the past decade. Whether it is the work of Andy Hargreaves and Dennis Shirley in The Fourth Way, or the work of Michael Fullan outlining the wrong and right drivers for reform cited earlier, or the thought-provoking work of Yong Zhao on the purpose and functions of an effective education system, there has been a shift in educational leadership thinking to capture the hearts and unifying purpose of education. It is a big-picture approach to educational leadership and reform that sees greater value in unity and viewing the process of education and reform as a whole.

> *Horizons draw our eyes towards the distance. They define the very edge of our existing vision. Spread all around the compass, they provide points of focus to possible ways forward. Horizons are not destinations. They provide landmarks on a journey that offer their own viewpoints and that can (but do not always) motivate travelers to find and forge their paths ahead. As German philosopher Hans-Georg Gadamer advised us, "Applying this to the thinking mind, we speak of narrowness of horizon, of the possible expansion of horizon, of the opening up of new horizons, and so forth." 4 Horizons are our future starting points. They are, at their best, our geography of hope.*
>
> —Andy Hargreaves and Dennis Shirley[1]

They go on to cite the example once again of Finland (yes, I know, but bear with me. And plus, they do things well in Finland),

> *In Finland, the state steers but does not prescribe in detail the national curriculum. Trusted teams of highly qualified teachers write much of the curriculum at the level of the municipality, in ways that adjust to the students they know*

best. In schools characterized by an uncanny calmness, teachers say they feel responsible for all children in their school—not just those in their own classes, subjects, or grade levels. And they collaborate quietly on all their students' behalf in cultures of trust, cooperation, and responsibility.[2]

—Andy Hargreaves and Dennis Shirley

Remember those words, cultures of trust, cooperation, and responsibility. These words become key in understanding how the education reform movement has become a movement of collaboration. It has been moving away from individual answers and also individual actors to move the system as a whole closer toward its potential. One doesn't create a whole system change by solely focusing on the individual or by focusing only on what their job title states. Whole system change comes about by changing the system of change. And the system is made up of all of us.

We are all actors, stakeholders, and drivers of change and we are all recipients of that change. By extolling and purposefully unifying each of us around what school could and should be and showing that we all have a role to play, this new form of whole system change becomes a collective push.

Teachers and principals view the principal's role as being one of a "society of experts" whose task is to draw knowledge and ideas out of colleagues rather than driving initiatives through them. Indeed, if the principal should fall sick or have a prolonged absence for any reason, teachers say they simply take over the school because it belongs to all of them.

In the city of Tampere, many principals have taken on significant responsibilities across the municipality as well as within their own schools, prompting them to develop and distribute greater leadership capacity within their schools while they are working systemwide. More than this, the principals recognized they are not just responsible for children in their own schools, but rather are jointly responsible for all the children of Tampere—for the future of the city and the civic pride they invest in it. If resources are lacking for a needed initiative, a principal contacts colleagues who respond, "We have a little bit extra—would you like some of ours?"[3]

—Andy Hargreaves and Dennis Shirley

Michael Fullan, as we highlighted earlier, has echoed this approach on tackling system reform in education by reframing our purposes and drivers. *"The new right drivers, by contrast,"* as Fullan articulates, *"capture and propel the human spirit."*[4]

Systemness (wholeness) instead of Fragmentation (inertia)
Social Intelligence (limitless) over Machine Intelligence (careless)

Wellbeing and Learning (essence) in place of Academics Obsession (selfish)
Equality Investments (dignity), not Austerity (ruthless)

> *Systemness is to systemic what coherence is to alignment. The latter element in each pair is rational while the former element in the twosome is subjective. Systemness is within individuals and groups; it is how they think, act and feel about the system. It is, if you like, within the human not the bloodless paradigm where emotions and motivation reside . . . "systemness" is defined as the sense that people have at all levels of the system that they are indeed the system. This means they have a responsibility to interact with, learn from, contribute to and be a living member of the system as it evolves.*
>
> —Michael Fullan[5]

Yong Zhao echoes similar needs for a broader, more human-centric, diverse, and ultimately nonconformist education system.

> *The divide between developing individuals and citizens can be at odds with each other when societies demand uniform thinking, homogenous beliefs and values, and identical abilities and knowledge for all citizens, while individuals possess different interests and passions, diverse beliefs and values, and distinct talents. However, this divide is removed when a society cherishes differences, values diversity, and respects individuality. Today, diversity and differences are not only an ideal pursuit but, more important, a necessity for any society to advance in the face of technological advances that are increasingly rendering sameness, homogeneity, and uniformity in thinking, beliefs, and abilities obsolete.*[6]
>
> —Yong Zhao[7]

An education system that seeks to create uniform pathways, and rids itself of its human-ness, will do more harm to both the individual and society. Such frameworks too often stifle innovation, ignore inherent talents, and relegate education to a set of facts to be learned or a series of skills to be performed.

> *This new paradigm of education requires a complete rethinking about every aspect of the entire education system, from the definition of quality to accountability measures, from curriculum to pedagogy, from learning settings to evaluation and assessment, and from selection to credentialing. The goal of the existing paradigm is about ensuring all students achieving the same outcomes. All aspects of the education system have been built around that goal. Therefore, this new paradigm requires transforming the education system so that it becomes capable of perceiving and educating children as unique individuals.*[8]

We can do better, we should do better, and we are starting to see the shift from standardized but siloed approaches in education to ones that are unified but nurturing to the individual learner and their needs. We learn this in the same way by knocking down walls, sharing ideas, and discussing purpose(s). We do it by collaboration and connection.

WEAVING

"Weaving" is a term that has arisen in recent years to outline an approach for ensuring or developing cross-collaboration, collective growth, and shared learning. One of the key proponents of this work has been Ross Hall who founded the Weaving Lab. Stemming out of the idea that we work and live too often restricted by siloes and separate by fragmentation The Weaving Lab sort to share and develop methods that improve the process of shared learning or weaving.

> As a learning community, we are exploring and innovating ways to cultivate our collective learning. For us, learning is an ongoing process of "becoming" the systems we wish to see.... We are community builders, network conveners, social innovators, and change-makers who want to experiment and learn how to become better weavers.[9]

In a talk Ross delivered in 2020 to an audience of educators, community activists, and change makers, he outlined the process and purpose of Weaving.

> In my opinion, we fundamentally need to transform the very purpose and practice of education, so that the central focus—what we pay attention to—is the holistic empowerment of every young person to live for universal well-being. That's a huge undertaking. So how do we create change?
>
> The first thing we believe is that we have to find those people who are already creating change, and we have to find more of them, and we have to connect with each other. Then we have to align to a North Star. We have to agree that there is a shared Purpose, that we have a shared goal. And beyond that, we then need to come together to form teams to collaborate with each other, and we need to connect those teams into teams of teams, each of whom is working to empower young people.
>
> These are teams working in every community, around every school, and involving every home. But teams also that are involving policymakers, the unions, the teacher training providers, etc. We need to, in other words, not just align to a North Star but share learnings and share opportunities, and share resources, and share experiences together. And beyond that, we also need to think

systemically. We've got to stop patching up problems. We've got to get into the source of the problem. We've got to get into changing systemic mechanisms, the policies, and rules, and incentives, that drive our education systems and wider systems. And beyond that we've got to go even deeper to get into changing the mindsets. Our mindsets which fuel and bring to life our education systems. We've got to change our attitudes, and our values, and our beliefs, and what we pay attention to, and what we talk about.

In other words, we've got to change our awareness, and our consciousness, in order to bring about this massive transformation. We've got to move from a very mechanistic understanding of education—a factory-like or machine-like model of education in which kids come in one end in batches, and are spewed out the other end. And we've got to create more human, adaptable, fluid, ecosystems—learning ecosystems, empowering learning ecosystems. And this process of creating empowering learning ecosystems is a process that we call weaving.

Weaving is a new leadership capacity that we need to adopt. Weaving is about aligning people to a common North Star. Weaving is about collaborating. It's about being systemic. It's about empowering everyone to live for universal well-being.

—Ross Hall[10]

And as Ross alluded to this must start with a change of mindset. A change from receiving an education to experiencing and crafting an education. A change from being a recipient of decisions to being an active player and stakeholder in our communities and our world. A change from seeing things as individual elements to understanding how we are all connected, interconnected.

NETWORKS AND WORKING THOSE NETS

The rise of weaving has been accompanied, or perhaps instigated by a growing desire and need to network and learn from others. The rise of the internet and the explosion of accessibility via mobile phones has certainly helped this, but it has also been accompanied by a desire from educators to share and learn from one another.

The annual conference or professional development day where professionals can share expertise has now gone virtual and is 24/7. EdChat, the Twitter hashtag, and weekly education discussion were started by Tom Whitby, Steven Anderson, and Shelly Sanchez Terrell, in 2009 as a way to use social media as a construct for sharing and discussing educational issues and craft.

The initial desire was simple enough, but it has proven to be a core construct in North American, and in fact global, educational dialogue.

> What we hoped to accomplish was to give transparency to education issues. Since it has continually run for over a dozen years fostering hundreds of thousands of tweets and influencing hundreds, if not thousands of blog posts, I think we have accomplished that goal.
>
> —Tom Whitby, interview, March 18, 2023

Though attendance during the weekly EdChat cannot be tracked, the number of tweets and retweets often gets into the thousands per hour, making it one of the most popular and frequented Twitter groups focusing on education.

It has helped grow educational professional learning across social media as a driving force, vastly usurping the number of educators attending conferences, or conducting more formal professional development. It is educational learning by, and for, the professionals without much of a middleman or go-between.

EdChat may have been a precursor, but it wasn't and hasn't been the only one. What we have seen over the past decade and especially during the Covid years has been an infusion of networks, many targeting different aspects areas of the system or sector and each acting to learn from others—working those nets of networking.

Anthony Mackay and Valerie Hannon established the Global Education Leaders Partnership, or GELP, in 2009 stemming out of the Innovation Unit in the UK. Initially comprising of leaders from fewer than a dozen countries, it now regularly hosts gatherings, symposiums, learning sessions, with a multitude of leaders from across varied countries, spanning the global north and south. It is succeeding in becoming a global "network of networks" bringing together diverse international initiatives whose goal is to transform education to meet the needs of the future. Rather than adjust or tinker with the current systems and their inherent issues, GELP is looking to transform education, and via this, transform the way other sectors, both private and public, interact with education. Their initial charge a dozen years ago was to "question what societal, environmental and technological change meant for our school systems, in terms of why, what and how we educate"[11] and as we have all witnessed over the past few years, this call or need to transform is now an unavoidable part of educational progress, and as Anthony (Tony) Mackay stated recently perhaps also for humanity.

> I can't recall a time when the discourse, the debate, the dialogue about learning has been so intense. If I think about a time now, that's the equivalent of the shift that I was experiencing in the '70s, it's now. This is the moment where people, I

> think, are saying learning is the fundamental challenge that we have and just to kind of capture the significance of it, this is learning at all levels. This is learning for global sustainability, this is learning for the sustainability of our own societies and economies, this is learning for the relationship between ourselves and all others and it's learning for a deeper understanding of self. To me, this is the moment where learning and the way in which we think about the future of learning is going to be so crucial to our own sustainability, globally and, obviously, as a human race.[12]

As with many of these networks they seek to raise educator agency and to infuse education planning and policy with the voice of educators, as opposed to that of politicians. Growing agency and seeking educator and educational purpose in policy.

For the past almost dozen years, Saku Tuominen via his K12 innovation organization HundrED has sought to illuminate the hundred—hence the name—most outstanding global education initiatives annually. It is an effort to democratize education by sharing and learning across varying cultures and countries. The idea is to both spread great ideas but also to establish a way—a network—where educators can share and learn from each other. Not everything may be applicable, and not everything showcased may work in other regions, but the idea is to promote sharing and highlight exceptional ideas that have made it to practice.

> [T]he world of education is full of great innovations. Unfortunately, they seldom manage to spread around the world. HundrED's mission is to help schools change. We do this by seeking and sharing inspiring innovations in K12 education.[13]

HundrED is a Finnish organization and originated by promoting the various initiatives underway across Finland—a country well known and well-regarded in education circles. And somewhat unsurprisingly the idea or concept of wholeness arises when Saku discusses the influence of Finnish education.

> Many countries ask us how to be successful too, and want to achieve similar results, but when we tell them that it requires implementing all of the elements that we use—including less homework, shorter days, more personal freedom—at this point they say, "no, we're not looking for that part," but we explain that you can't achieve one without the other.[14]

You can't achieve one without the other. You can't focus only on one thing and expect the sane results. You can't dissect that part you may happen to like and agree with and ignore the rest.

The question that each of these groups, and there are many more, are tackling with is how to make networking part of the process and part of the system. How do we continue to share expertise, ideas, solutions during times when there isn't an immediate crisis? How do we make learning about learning be a ubiquitous part of every system?

While Covid caused the immediate shut down of many schools and systems, it also inadvertently manifested the need for a new form of sharing and learning. Online was the simplest and, for many, the only way to cross pollinate ideas and because of the crisis there were many seeking immediate ideas and help.

This has continued as we have entered a post-Covid period. Not only is online learning considered differently than it was pre-Covid, the act of sharing has become much more mainstream. People are more open to sharing ideas and from hearing from others. It is as if our shutdown has allowed us to reconnect—but in a different form. It has opened a need that many educators didn't know existed. That is not to say that online is the only or the best way to share but rather that it has allowed many more people to interact and be a part of networks and networking.

Prior to Covid many global education events were exclusive in every sense of the word. They required invitations. They required the funds to pay for registration, for the travel, and for the hotel accommodations. Many of these events did not intend to be restrictive but were precisely because of the location, cost, and the practical need to be exclusive. During Covid events were cancelled, postponed, or they went online.

Groups that previously were consistently underrepresented in many events and discussions—particularly those from minority cultural groups, remote locations, and particularly those from the Global South—were now suddenly finding that were more able to be "at the table." Yes, people still need the invitation, but online audiences don't need seats, nor do they need to be fed or housed. Capacity was much less an issue and access often came down to having a mobile phone or internet connection. Not perfect but certainly an improvement and less of an impediment. The barriers to inclusion were being reduced.

Suddenly we were hearing from a more varied and diverse set of educators and many more were hearing and discussing the ideas.

T4 Education was launched by Vikas Pota in 2020 as a response to the pandemic and the need for educators to access information. Many were thrown into the "new world" of online virtual learning and were not prepared to respond adequately to the change.

The initial idea was to bring "together a global community of schools and educators from around the world, who, when faced with school closures due to the pandemic wanted to know how to navigate the 'new normal' and seek to advance their agency to improve education for all."[15]

This has quickly morphed into an ongoing endeavor to help learn from others and to surface best practices, build strong schools, and enhance school culture to transform teaching and learning.

Their first global conference focused on four key areas—leadership, collaboration, well-being, and technology—and the focus and the target soon stuck, hence T4.

What they have done in a short time is both exemplary and a bell weather for what is possible and needed. After launching at the start of the pandemic, they soon held their first global conference, with over 100,000 teachers registered to attend. One hundred thousand educators from across the world who only required internet capability. T4 Education exposed a need and proved that educators are willing—needing—to network.

Hopefully one of the major fundamental changes that education will witness over the next decade will be the end of educators figuratively and literally shutting their classroom doors. We learn better in collaboration. We grow better together. We perform better by sharing.

As Vikas stated in a recent conversation, "We're building the world's largest community of teachers and schools because the world we want to see in which every child receives their birthright of a good education cannot wait to be built by top-down reform—it must be powered by grassroots change."[16]

And in some ways bringing all these elements and facets and themes together is the project LearningPlanet created in 2020 by the Learning Planet Institute and UNESCO. This open alliance has established a series of venues and events that bring together a "growing community of diverse game changers and institutions learning to take care of oneself, others and the planet."[17] It is aiming to transform education, via the connection and collaboration of changemakers, for the benefit of the planet. It is whole-istic in its endeavors, and also in its aims.

And a prime example of this would be their LearningPlanet Circles that bring together both individuals and organizations, all committed to the same thematic priorities and outcomes.

Take a look at the current themes and the current organizations involved and you get the idea.

Youth Empowerment Circle
Co-led by LearningPlanet, CAP-2030 and Catalyst 2030
Collaborating to connect inspirational youth game changers and initiatives across health, sustainability, rights and education.

Teachers for the Planet Circle
Co-led by LearningPlanet, the Aga Khan Foundation, and Teach for All

The official long-term road to COP28 for the advancement of climate action and leadership through education: a global community of practice for members of the Teachers for the Planet programme—teachers, school and system-level leaders in climate and education who meet throughout the year to discuss and debate solutions for the future of the planet.

Ubuntu Learning Circle
Co-led by LearningPlanet and The Club of Rome
Bringing together a small working group of committed actors who are active in place-based learning and sustainability initiatives in Africa.

Imagination Circle
Co-led by LearningPlanet and AIME
Bringing together people exploring and testing imagination programmes, workshops and curriculums inside formal and informal education systems.

Transitions in Higher Education Circle
Co-led by Co-led by LearningPlanet and University Design Institute (ASU)
Charting possible avenues for collaboration between higher education institutions, to collectively shape a vision of higher education for the 21st century. In circle sessions, members share their experiences implementing new ways of learning and doing research to better address the challenges of our time.[18]

What they are developing, as are T4, GELP, Weaving Lab, HundrED, and EdChat, are spaces—not places—where people and organizations can work together collaboratively, across countries and amongst cultures, each battling different systems to change the world of education and learning and hopefully change the world for the better at the same time.

These are not the only players in the networking space, but they are all changemakers in how networking gets done and how meaningful change happens. We can learn together, and we can learn as a whole. Seeing or doing things in isolation is no longer justified.

NOTES

1. Hargreaves, A., & Shirley, D., *The Fourth Way: The Inspiring Future for Educational Change*, Corwin Press, 2009, p. 49.
2. Ibid., p. 53.
3. Ibid., p. 54.
4. Fullan, M. (2021), Op Cit, p. 31.
5. Ibid., p. 33.

6. *The Learning Compact Renewed: Whole Child for the Whole World*, 2020, Op Cit, p. 31.

7. Zhao, Y., *What Works May Hurt: Side Effects in Education*, Teachers College Press, 2018.

8. *The Learning Compact Renewed: Whole Child for the Whole World*, 2020, Op Cit, p. 32.

9. *What We Do At The Weaving Lab—Collaborative System Change*, The Weaving Lab, December 9, 2021. Retrieved January 8, 2023, from https://weavinglab.org/about-the-weaving-lab/.

10. Hall, R., *Empowering Youth to Live for Wellbeing*, The Love Behind Food Summit, 2020. Retrieved January 15, 2023, from https://www.youtube.com/watch?v=X7Gmo7RqNTg.

11. Global Education Leaders Partnership, Training, n.d. Retrieved March 20, 2023, from https://sites.google.com/uldtraining.com/gelp.

12. *Tony Mackay Knows the Power of Networks and Partnerships*, Interview with Anthony Mackay, Victorian Academy of Teaching and Learning, February 12, 2019. Retrieved March 20, 2023, from https://www.academy.vic.gov.au/learning-resources/tony-mackay-knows-power-networks-and-partnerships.

13. Cocking, S., *Saku Tuominen's Hundred Global Education Initiative, Aiming to Shake Up Global Education*, The Irish Times, December 10, 2016. Retrieved January 15, 2023, https://irishtechnews.ie/saku-tuominens-hundred-global-education-initiative-aiming-to-shake-up-global-education/.

14. Ibid.

15. *About T4 Education—Thoughts from Our Founder*. Retrieved January 15, 2023, from https://t4.education/about-t4.

16. Conversation with Vikas Pota, April 18, 2023.

17. LearningPlanet, About, n.d. Retrieved March 20, 2023, from https://www.learning-planet.org/.

18. LearningPlanet, Circles, n.d. Retrieved March 20, 2023, from https://www.learning-planet.org/circles/.

Chapter 9

The Whole Is Greater than the Sum of Its Parts

The quote translated from Aristotle and used often incorrectly across many contexts fundamentally evokes the idea that the parts together make something more than themselves. The whole is more than each of the pieces.

> *To return to the difficulty which has been stated with respect both to definitions and to numbers, what is the cause of their unity? In the case of all things which have several parts and in which the totality is not, as it were, a mere heap, but the whole is something beside the parts, there is a cause; for even in bodies contact is the cause of unity in some cases, and in others viscosity or some other such quality.*
>
> —Aristotle[1]

It is still the most appropriate definition of what I am getting at in this book. If we dissect and examine each piece as a separate entity, we lose what makes the whole special, unique, and often beneficial. The interactions between the pieces, the ways that each piece benefits another, and the new entity or entities that are formed by combining the pieces. When we dissect, we too often remove that piece from its purpose or at a minimum reduce its function.

It is true of our world, our ecosystems, ourselves. It is also true of our systems, and none is more guilty of that than education. We cut, we exchange, we swap out, we rearrange what is being taught. Then we—like Frankenstein's monster—try to reassemble parts of it, piece by piece. And then we go through the cycle or process again. It is a bit like walking up and down Escher's staircase and discovering that even though we've traveled we haven't actually gotten anywhere. We attach accountability measures to the pieces but too often don't appreciate the whole of what should be being taught—and potentially learned by our students.

The good news in this world of pieces and siloes that we find ourselves in is that the remedy begins with our perspective and our curiosity.

Much of what I am alluding to here is as much an approach and mindset, as it is a process. Or it is, at a minimum, commenced, and maintained by mindset. The mindset is that "we are connected" and that "when we separate, we run the risk of losing what is core." We risk losing that what links, what binds, and what makes something function.

The mindset is that the whole is greater than its parts.

By keeping this front of mind and by referring back to the whole we maintain the existence of the whole. When we myopically focus only on the parts and hold them up to be all that is important, we lose the context, the reason, and the purpose of what is being learned or at least what is trying to be taught.

The first steps for any of this are to change our perspective and in doing so question our mindset. By questioning, we ask ourselves what is it that we are seeking and then subsequently is there a better way. If we are seeking the memorization of discreet pieces of content or skill, then perhaps the way we have approached teaching works. But if we are seeking to teach the whole person and to understand how they and their world interacts, how what they learn in one subject area aligns to another, how art corresponds to games, how history aligns with literature, how science is embedded within music, how one's emotions connect to one's functions, how one's actions help and foster the community, and how we are greater than our parts, then we must also develop learning environments that complement and enhance the whole.

NOTE

1. Translation of Aristotle's Metaphysics Book VIII, 1045a.8–10. Retrieved January 15, 2023, https://se-scholar.com/se-blog/2017/6/23/who-said-the-whole-is-greater-than-the-sum-of-the-parts.

Bibliography

Abrams, R., *Strategies: Entrepreneurs Preventing the Next Katrina*, USA Today, August, 2015. Retrieved January 8, 2023, from https://www.usatoday.com/story/money/columnist/abrams/2015/08/28/strategies-entrepreneurs-preventing-next-katrina/32456567/

Alexander, H., *"It's a Trojan Horse for CRT": Now Furious Parents Push Back against Social Emotional Learning (SEL) Being Taught in Schools, Claiming Its Promotion of "Diversity" Is More Evidence of Government Indoctrination*, Daily Mail, November 16, 2021. Retrieved January 8, 2023, from https://www.dailymail.co.uk/news/article-10206207/Youre-actually-advertising-suicide-Parents-push-against-Social-Emotional-Learning-school.html

Allensworth, D., & Kolbe, L., *The Comprehensive School Health Program*, Journal of School Health, Wiley, December 1987. Retrieved January 8, 2023, from https://onlinelibrary.wiley.com/doi/abs/10.1111/j.1746-1561.1987.tb03183.x

ASCD, Educational Leadership Magazine archives. Retrieved January 8, 2023.

ASCD, *The Learning Compact Redefined: A Call to Action*, 2007. Retrieved January 8, 2023, from https://library.ascd.org/m/21e2f544234c3e97/original/WCC-Learning-Compact.pdf

ASCD, *The Learning Compact Renewed: Whole Child for the Whole World*, ASCD, 2020. Retrieved January 8, 2023, from http://files.ascd.org/pdfs/programs/WholeChildNetwork/2020-whole-child-network-learning-compact-renewed.pdf

ASCD and CDC, *Whole School, Whole Community, Whole Child: A Collaborative Approach to Learning and Health*, 2014.

Auto, H., *Public Service to Go from "Whole-of-Government" to "Whole-of-Nation,"* The Straits Times, May 9, 2018. Retrieved January 8, 2023, from https://www.straitstimes.com/politics/public-service-to-go-from-whole-of-government-to-whole-of-nation

Barrows, H. S., & Tamblyn, R. M., *Problem-based Learning: An Approach to Medical Education*, Springer Publishing Company, 1980. Retrieved March 18, 2023, from https://app.nova.edu/toolbox/instructionalproducts/edd8124/fall11/1980-BarrowsTamblyn-PBL.pdf

Blad, E., *There's Pushback to Social-Emotional Learning. Here's What Happened in One State*, Education Week, June 23, 2022. Retrieved January 8, 2023, from https://www.edweek.org/education/theres-pushback-to-social-emotional-learning-heres-what-happened-in-one-state/2020/02

Boaler, J., *Learning from Teaching: Exploring the Relationship between Reform Curriculum and Equity*, Journal for Research in Mathematics Education, 33(4), 239–58, 2002.

Bonamici, Fitzpatrick Introduce Bipartisan Resolution in Support of Whole Child Approach to Education, Congresswoman Suzanne Bonamici, June 21, 2022. Retrieved January 8, 2023, from https://bonamici.house.gov/media/press-releases/bonamici-fitzpatrick-introduce-bipartisan-resolution-support-whole-child

Bordoloi, S., & Parkes, J., *Applying a Whole School Approach*, UNGEI, December 9, 2021. Retrieved January 8, 2023, from https://www.ungei.org/blog-post/applying-whole-school-approach

Brown, N., *More Than Fun and Games—Play Matters*, Huffington Post, December 7, 2017. Retrieved January 8, 2023, from https://www.huffpost.com/entry/more-than-fun-and-games-p_b_5997688

Butler, T., *Cane Toads Increasingly a Problem in Australia*. Mongabay Environmental News, April 1, 2005. Retrieved January 8, 2023, from https://news.mongabay.com/2005/04/cane-toads-increasingly-a-problem-in-australia/

Camargo, L. A., *Education, What Is It Really?* LinkedIn, August 13, 2018. Retrieved January 8, 2023, from https://www.linkedin.com/pulse/20141028130802-9247365-education-what-is-it-really?trk=public_profile_article_vie

Center for Drug Evaluation and Research, *Drug Recalls*, U.S. Food and Drug Administration, n.d. Retrieved January 8, 2023, from https://www.fda.gov/drugs/drug-safety-and-availability/drug-recalls

Cigna's Whole Health Vision, Cigna Global, n.d. Retrieved January 8, 2023, from https://www.cignaglobal.com/blog/whole-health/cignas-whole-health-vision?irclickid=3qOx143I4xyIROCWS30uaQoxUkDRGcyJRUBPyY0&irgwc=1&utm_content=296083_ONLINE_TRACKING_LINK_&utm_campaign=106140&utm_source=123201_adgoal+gmbh&utm_medium=affiliate

Cocking, S., *Saku Tuominen's Hundred Global Education Initiative, Aiming to Shake Up Global Education*, The Irish Times, December 10, 2016. Retrieved January 15, 2023, from https://irishtechnews.ie/saku-tuominens-hundred-global-education-initiative-aiming-to-shake-up-global-education/

Dewey, J., *Individual Psychology and Education*, The Philosopher, XII, 1934.

Dewey, J., *My Pedagogic Creed*, School Journal, 54(3), 77–80, 1897.

Doris Pilkington Garimara, State Library of Western Australia, n.d. Retrieved January 8, 2023, from https://slwa.wa.gov.au/whats-on/awards-fellowships/western-australian-writers-hall-fame/doris-pilkington-garimara

EdWeek Leaders To Learn From, *Catching Up with Past Leaders to Learn From: Where They Are Now*, EdWeek, February 16, 2022. Retrieved January 8, 2023, from https://www.edweek.org/leaders/leadership/catching-up-with-past-leaders-to-learn-from-where-they-are-now/2022/02

Ehrenfreund, M., *Finland's New Plan to Change School Means Combining Subjects*, The Washington Post, November 25, 2021. Retrieved January 8, 2023, from https://

www.washingtonpost.com/news/wonk/wp/2015/03/24/finlands-radical-new-plan-to-change-school-means-an-end-to-math-and-history-class/

Fan, R. *Thalidomide: "The Biggest Man-Made Medical Disaster Ever,"* Medium, August 3, 2021. Retrieved January 8, 2023, from https://medium.com/frame-of-reference/thalidomide-the-biggest-man-made-medical-disaster-ever-2988096e7716

Foshay, A. W., *The Curriculum Matrix: Transcendence and Mathematics*, 1991. https://files.ascd.org/staticfiles/ascd/pdf/journals/ed_update/eu201207_infographic.pdf

Freire, P., *Pedagogy of the Oppressed*, Penguin Classics, 1972.

Frey, N., Fisher, D., & Smith, D., *All Learning Is Social and Emotional: The Hidden Curriculum*, ASCD, 2018.

Fullan, M., *Choosing the Wrong Drivers for Whole System Reform*, CSE Seminar Series Paper 204, Centre for Strategic Education, Melbourne, 2011.

Fullan, M., *The Right Drivers for Whole System Success*, Centre for Strategic Education, 2021.

Ganesan, V., Lam, Y., & Lin, D., *How Singapore Is Harnessing Design to Transform Government Services*, McKinsey & Company, June 23, 2021. Retrieved January 8, 2023, from https://www.mckinsey.com/industries/public-and-social-sector/our-insights/how-singapore-is-harnessing-design-to-transform-government-services

García, L. E., & Thornton, O., *"No Child Left Behind" Has Failed*, The Washington Post, February 13, 2015. Retrieved January 8, 2023, from https://www.washingtonpost.com/opinions/no-child-has-failed/2015/02/13/8d619026-b2f8-11e4-827f-93f454140e2b_story.html

Global Education Futures, About Us, n.d. Retrieved March 30, 2023, from https://globaledufutures.org/about_us

Global Education Leaders Partnership, Training, n.d. Retrieved March 20, 2023, from https://sites.google.com/uldtraining.com/gelp

Gold Standard Project Based Learning, PBLWorks, n.d. Retrieved March 18, 2023, from https://www.pblworks.org/what-is-pbl/gold-standard-project-design

Gordon, S., *Spark Talk—Sal Gordon*. Retrieved January 8, 2023, from https://www.youtube.com/watch?v=4tIbY65FkJU

Green School International, HundrED, June 29, 2020. Retrieved January 8, 2023, from https://hundred.org/en/innovations/green-school-international

Griffith, D., *ASCD Policy Priorities/Everybody's Talking about the Whole Child*, ASCD, October 1, 2019. Retrieved January 8, 2023, from https://www.ascd.org/el/articles/everybodys-talking-about-the-whole-child

Hall, R., *Empowering Youth to Live for Wellbeing*, The Love Behind Food Summit, 2020. Retrieved January 15, 2023, from https://www.youtube.com/watch?v=X7Gmo7RqNTg

Hargreaves, A., & Shirley, D., *Wellbeing in Schools*, ASCD, 2022.

Hargreaves, A., & Shirley, D., *The Fourth Way: The Inspiring Future for Educational Change*, Corwin Press, 2009.

Haun, J., Melillo, C., Cotner, B., McMahon-Grenz, J., & Paykel, J., *Evaluating a Whole Health Approach to Enhance Veteran Care: Exploring the Staff Experience*, Journal of Veterans Studies, May 27, 2021. Retrieved January 8, 2023, from https://journal-veterans-studies.org/article/10.21061/jvs.v7i1.201/

How "Old People's Home for 4 Year Olds" Might Force a Shake-Up in Social Care, University of Bath, July 25, 2018. Retrieved January 8, 2023, from https://www.bath.ac.uk/case-studies/how-old-peoples-home-for-4-year-olds-might-force-a-shake-up-in-social-care/

How We Get There: Whole School Effort, Trauma Sensitive Schools, January 31, 2019. Retrieved January 8, 2023, from https://traumasensitiveschools.org/trauma-and-learning/how-we-get-there-whole-school-effort/; https://www.ascd.org/el/all

International Security Sector Advisory Team (ISSAT), *Whole-of-Government Approach (WGA)*, International Security Sector Advisory Team (ISSAT), n.d. Retrieved January 8, 2023, from https://issat.dcaf.ch/Learn/Resource-Library/SSR-Glossary/Whole-of-Government-Approach-WGA

ISSG Database: Impact Information for Styela Clava, n.d. Retrieved January 8, 2023, from http://issg.org/database/species/impact_info.asp?si=951

Ivey, B. K., *Gov. Kay Ivey's 2020 State of the State Address*, Alabama Political Reporter, February 5, 2020. Retrieved January 8, 2023, from https://www.alreporter.com/2020/02/04/gov-kay-iveys-2020-state-of-the-state-address/

Jackson, P., *Life in Classrooms*, New York: Holt, Rine- hart and Winston, 1968.

Johnson, C., *Is It Too Late to Bring the Red Fox under Control?* The Conversation, January 5, 2023. Retrieved January 8, 2023, from https://theconversation.com/is-it-too-late-to-bring-the-red-fox-under-control-11299

King, M. L. Jr., *The Purpose of Education*, Maroon Tiger, January–February 1947.

Kohn, A., *The Trouble with "Back to Basics,"* n.d. Retrieved January 8, 2023, from https://www.alfiekohn.org/teaching/ttwbtbats.htm

Lassman, A., *Flying Rivers of the Amazon Rainforest—A Critical Rain Generator for the Planet*, Pachamama Alliance's Blog, n.d. Retrieved January 8, 2023, from https://blog.pachamama.org/flying-rivers-of-the-amazon-rainforest-a-critical-rain-generator-for-the-planet

LearningPlanet, About, n.d. Retrieved March 20, 2023, from https://www.learning-planet.org/

LearningPlanet, Circles, n.d. Retrieved March 20, 2023, from https://www.learning-planet.org/circles/

Lovett, I., *Teacher's Death Exposes Tensions in Los Angeles*, The New York Times, November 9, 2010. Retrieved January 8, 2023, from https://www.nytimes.com/2010/11/10/education/10teacher.html

Lupkin, S., *One-Third of New Drugs Had Safety Problems after FDA Approval*, NPR, May 9, 2017. Retrieved January 8, 2023, from https://www.npr.org/sections/health-shots/2017/05/09/527575055/one-third-of-new-drugs-had-safety-problems-after-fda-approval

Madness, *Our House*, Stiff Records, 12 November 1982.

Maslow, A. H., *A Theory of Human Motivation*, Psychological Review, 50, 1943. Retrieved December 20, 2023, from http://psychclassics.yorku.ca/Maslow/motivation.htm

McAnulty, H., *History Talking: Oral History Group Recalls Hare-Raising Experiences*, Central Western Daily, September 14, 2014. Retrieved January 8, 2023, from https://www.centralwesterndaily.com.au/story/2557856/history-talking-oral-history-group-recalls-hare-raising-experiences/?cs=103

McClure, T., *Climate Crisis Pushes Albatross "Divorce" Rates Higher—Study*, The Guardian, November 24, 2021. Retrieved December 8, 2023, from https://www.theguardian.com/environment/2021/nov/24/climate-crisis-pushes-albatross-divorce-rates-higher-study

Michael Fullan: Author, Speaker, Educational Consultant—Michael Fullan, n.d. Retrieved January 8, 2023, from https://michaelfullan.ca/wp-content/uploads/2021/03/Fullan-CSE-Leading-Education-Series-01-2021R2-compressed.pdf

Mississippi Whole Schools, December 12, 2022. Retrieved January 8, 2023, from https://mswholeschools.org/

Mitchell, T., *In Their Own Words, Americans Describe the Struggles and Silver Linings of the Covid-19 Pandemic*, Pew Research Center, January 5, 2023. Retrieved January 8, 2023, from https://www.pewresearch.org/2021/03/05/in-their-own-words-americans-describe-the-struggles-and-silver-linings-of-the-covid-19-pandemic/

Munro O'Brien, J., *It's a Dog of a Way to Get High but Queensland Pooches Are Lapping up Hallucinogenic Sweat from Cane Toads*, The Courier Mail, December 16, 2013. Retrieved January 8, 2023, from https://www.couriermail.com.au/news/queensland/its-a-dog-of-a-way-to-get-high-but-queensland-pooches-are-lapping-up-hallucinogenic-sweat-from-cane-toads/news-story/854464b203fcbf60e129dd0c85cbc914

Nelson, E., *Building School Community through Physical Activity*, Edutopia, November 19, 2019. Retrieved January 8, 2023, from https://www.edutopia.org/article/building-school-community-through-physical-activity

Nicholas, S., & Downing, M. D., *Postmarket Safety Events among Therapeutics Approved by the FDA*, JAMA, May 9, 2017. Retrieved January 8, 2023, from https://jamanetwork.com/journals/jama/fullarticle/2625319

Pappas, S., *As Schools Cut Recess, Kids' Learning Will Suffer, Experts Say*, LiveScience, August 14, 2011. Retrieved January 8, 2023, from https://www.livescience.com/15555-schools-cut-recess-learning-suffers.html

Pavel Luksha on the Future of Skills, Getting Smart Podcast with Tom Vander Ark, March 31, 2021. Retrieved March 30, 2023, from https://www.gettingsmart.com/podcast/pavel-luksha-on-the-future-of-skills/

Pavitra, K. S., Chandrashekar, C. R., & Choudhury, P., *Creativity and Mental Health: A Profile of Writers and Musicians*, Indian Journal of Psychiatry, 49(1), 34–43, 2007, https://doi.org/10.4103/0019-5545.31516

PBL Engaging the Disengaged, PBLWorks, January 4, 2019. Retrieved January 8, 2023, from https://www.pblworks.org/blog/pbl-engaging-disengaged

Petri, S., *Service-Learning Can Be the Bridge to Social Emotional Learning. Educators Should Embrace It*, EdSurge, September 6, 2022. Retrieved March 16, 2023, from https://www.edsurge.com/news/2022-09-06-service-learning-can-be-the-bridge-to-social-emotional-learning-educators-should-embrace-it

Pill, S., *Coach Development through Collaborative Action Research: An Australian Football Coach's Implementation of a Game Sense Approach*, University of Sydney Papers in HMHCE—Special Games Sense Edition, 2014.

PricewaterhouseCoopers, *Redefining Wellbeing in a Post-Pandemic World*, PwC, n.d. Retrieved January 8, 2023, from https://www.pwc.com/mt/en/publications/human-resources/redefining-wellbeing-in-a-post-pandemic-world.html

Proclamation 5197—Year of Excellence in Education, Ronald Reagan, n.d. Retrieved January 8, 2023, from https://www.reaganlibrary.gov/archives/speech/proclamation-5197-year-excellence-education

Project-Based Learning (PBL), Edutopia, https://www.edutopia.org/project-based-learning

Putnam, R. D., *Our Kids: The American Dream in Crisis*, Simon & Schuster Paperbacks, 2016.

Putnam, R., *Bowling Alone. The Collapse and Revival of American Community*, Simon & Schuster, 2000.

Rabbit-Proof Fence—Official Site—Miramax, Miramax Home Page, n.d. Retrieved January 8, 2023, from https://www.miramax.com/movie/rabbit-proof-fence/

Reilly, K., *Is Recess Important for Kids? Here's What the Research Says*, Time, October 23, 2017. Retrieved January 8, 2023, from https://time.com/4982061/recess-benefits-research-debate/

Rivlin, A., & Parkin, G., *Consumer Healthcare and Coronavirus: Three Trends That Will Continue to Drive Long-Term Industry Growth*, L.E.K. Consulting, February 16, 2021. Retrieved January 8, 2023, from https://www.lek.com/insights/ei/consumer-healthcare-and-coronavirus-three-trends-will-continue-drive-long-term-industry

Robert, D. Putnam, n.d. Retrieved January 8, 2023, from http://robertdputnam.com/

Robinson, S. K., *What Is Education For?* Edutopia, March 2, 2022. Retrieved January 8, 2023, from https://www.edutopia.org/article/what-education/

Roosevelt, E., *Good Citizenship: The Purpose of Education*, Pictorial Review, April 1930, archived in Yearbook of the National Society for the Study of Education, October 2008.

Sacks, O., *The Man Who Mistook His Wife for a Hat*, Picador, 2002.

Sahlberg, P., *How Germ Is Infecting Schools around the World?*, December 22, 2012. Retrieved January 8, 2023, from https://pasisahlberg.com/text-test/

Sahlberg, P., & Doyle, W., *Let the Children Play: For the Learning, Well-being, and Life Success of Every Child*, Oxford University Press, 2020.

Service Learning, Edutopia, n.d. Retrieved March 18, 2023, from https://www.edutopia.org/blog/what-heck-service-learning-heather-wolpert-gawron

Sharpe, M., & Spencer, A., *Many Americans Say They Have Shifted Their Priorities around Health and Social Activities during COVID-19*, Pew Research Center, January 5, 2023. Retrieved January 8, 2023, from https://www.pewresearch.org/fact-tank/2022/08/18/many-americans-say-they-have-shifted-their-priorities-around-health-and-social-activities-during-covid-19/

Simerman, J., *New Orleans' Lower 9th Ward Is Still Reeling from Hurricane Katrina's Damage 15 Years Later*, NOLA.com, August 29, 2020. Retrieved January 8, 2023, from https://www.nola.com/news/katrina/article_a192c350-ea0e-11ea-a863-2bc584f57987.html

Skerrett, P., *What Singapore Can Teach the U.S. about Responding to Covid-19*, STAT, March 23, 2020. Retrieved January 8, 2023, from https://www.statnews.com/2020/03/23/singapore-teach-united-states-about-covid-19-response/

Slade, S., *Why Do We Teach Sports?* Taylor & Francis, 2019. Retrieved January 8, 2023, from https://www.tandfonline.com/doi/abs/10.1080/07303084.1999.10605884

Slade, S., *Questioning Education: Moving from What & How to Why & Who*, Routledge Eye on Education, 2022.

Snyder, B. R., *The Hidden Curriculum*, Alfred A. Knopf, 1971.

Spiller, P., *Could Subjects Soon Be a Thing of the Past in Finland?* BBC News, May 28, 2017. Retrieved January 8, 2023, from https://www.bbc.com/news/world-europe-39889523

Subject Teaching in Finnish Schools Is Not Being Abolished, The Finnish National Board of Education—Current issues, n.d. Retrieved January 8, 2023, from https://web.archive.org/web/20151226185915/http:/www.oph.fi/english/current_issues/101/0/subject_teaching_in_finnish_schools_is_not_being_abolished

T4 Education—Thoughts from Our Founder. Retrieved January 15, 2023, from https://t4.education/about-t4

Tapper, J., *How the Elderly Can Help the Young—and Help Themselves*, The Guardian, January 5, 2019. Retrieved January 8, 2023, from https://www.theguardian.com/society/2019/jan/05/children-eldery-intergenerational-care-advantages

Teaching Kids to Stay Creative for Life | Joe Fatheree, United States | Global Teacher Prize. Retrieved January 8, 2023, from https://www.youtube.com/watch?v=j2zZCs1uSCw

The Amazon Approaches Its Tipping Point, The Nature Conservancy, August 20, 2020. Retrieved January 8, 2023, from https://www.nature.org/en-us/what-we-do/our-insights/perspectives/amazon-approaches-tipping-point/

The Teacher Solving Problems in a Remote Inuit Community | Maggie MacDonnell | Global Teacher Prize. Retrieved January 8, 2023, from https://www.youtube.com/watch?v=mh3gPBmauZg

Threat Abatement Plan for Predation by the European Red Fox—DCCEEW, n.d. Retrieved January 8, 2023, from https://www.dcceew.gov.au/sites/default/files/documents/tap-fox-background.pdf

Tony Mackay Knows the Power of Networks and Partnerships, Interview with Anthony Mackay.

Translation of Aristotle's Metaphysics Book VIII, 1045a.8–10. Retrieved January 15, 2023, from https://se-scholar.com/se-blog/2017/6/23/who-said-the-whole-is-greater-than-the-sum-of-the-parts

UNESCO, IBE Admin, *Whole School Approach*, International Bureau of Education, May 20, 2016. Retrieved January 8, 2023, from http://www.ibe.unesco.org/en/glossary-curriculum-terminology/w/whole-school-approach

US Centers for Disease Control and Prevention, *Social Determinants of Health at CDC*, Centers for Disease Control and Prevention, December 8, 2022. Retrieved January 8, 2023, from https://www.cdc.gov/about/sdoh/index.html

US Centers for Disease Control and Prevention, *Whole School, Whole Community, Whole Child (WSCC), U.S.*, Centers for Disease Control and Prevention, June 27, 2022. Retrieved January 8, 2023, from https://www.cdc.gov/healthyschools/wscc/index.htm

US Department of Education (ED), *Ed Strategic Plans and Annual Reports*, Home, July 28, 2022. Retrieved January 8, 2023, from https://www2.ed.gov/about/reports/strat/index.html

US Department of Education (ED), *Four Pillars of NCLB*, Home, December 19, 2005. Retrieved January 8, 2023, from https://www2.ed.gov/nclb/overview/intro/4pillars.html

US Department of Education, *U.S. Department of Education Emphasizes Importance of Full-Service Community Schools through Competitive Grant Program*, January 11, 2022. Retrieved January 8, 2023, from https://www.ed.gov/news/press-releases/us-department-education-emphasizes-importance-full-service-community-schools-through-competitive-grant-program

Victorian Academy of Teaching and Learning, February 12, 2019. Retrieved March 20, 2023, from https://www.academy.vic.gov.au/learning-resources/tony-mackay-knows-power-networks-and-partnerships

Visentin, L., *"Maths Must Change, Experts Push for More Problem-Solving in Maths Curriculum,"* The Sydney Morning Herald, April 11, 2021. Retrieved January 8, 2023, from https://www.smh.com.au/politics/federal/maths-must-change-experts-push-for-more-problem-solving-in-maths-curriculum-20210408-p57hj0.html

Viveros, F., & Ladha, A., *The "Lungs of the Earth" Are Really Its Heart: An Indigenous Cure to Save the Amazon*, The Correspondent, July 23, 2020. Retrieved January 8, 2023, from https://thecorrespondent.com/594/the-lungs-of-the-earth-are-really-its-heart-an-indigenous-cure-to-save-the-amazon

Vu, D., *The "Lungs of Our Planet" Are under Threat*, Discovery, June 22, 2020. Retrieved January 8, 2023, from https://www.discovery.com/nature/the--lungs-of-our-planet--are-under-threat

Wagner, A. C., *Couple Therapy with MDMA—Proposed Pathways of Action*, Frontiers in Psychology, 12, 2021, https://doi.org/10.3389/fpsyg.2021.733456

Walker, T., *What's the Purpose of Education? Public Doesn't Agree on the Answer*, NEA, n.d. Retrieved January 8, 2023, from https://www.nea.org/advocating-for-change/new-from-nea/whats-purpose-education-public-doesnt-agree-answer

Wallace-Wells, B., *How a Conservative Activist Invented the Conflict over Critical Race Theory*, The New Yorker, June 18, 2021. Retrieved January 8, 2023, from https://www.newyorker.com/news/annals-of-inquiry/how-a-conservative-activist-invented-the-conflict-over-critical-race-theory

Welch, C., *How Amazon Forest Loss Could Affect Water Supplies Far Away*, Environment, May 3, 2021. Retrieved January 8, 2023, from https://www.nationalgeographic.com/environment/article/how-cutting-the-amazon-forest-could-affect-weather

What We Do at the Weaving Lab—Collaborative System Change, The Weaving Lab, December 9, 2021. Retrieved January 8, 2023, from https://weavinglab.org/about-the-weaving-lab/

When to Teach Whole Versus Part Practice. Human Kinetics, n.d. Retrieved January 8, 2023, from https://us.humankinetics.com/blogs/excerpt/tagged/product-successful-coaching-4th-edition

Whole Health School of Medicine to become Alice L. Walton School of Medicine, Press release, June 30, 2022. Retrieved January 8, 2023, from https://www.alice-walton.org/whole-health-school-of-medicine-to-become-alice-l-walton-school-of-medicine

Whole School Sustainability Framework—Center for Green Schools, n.d. Retrieved January 8, 2023, from https://centerforgreenschools.org/sites/default/files/resource-files/Whole-School_Sustainability_Framework.pdf

Whole-School Approach: Mentally Healthy Schools, Heads Together Mentally Healthy Schools, n.d. Retrieved January 8, 2023, from https://mentallyhealthyschools.org.uk/whole-school-approach/

Whole-School Model, CARA, July 2, 2021. Retrieved January 8, 2023, from https://caranyc.org/whole-school-model/

Zagorski, N., *Psychedelic Therapy Hits Another Milestone, But Caution Urged,* Psychiatric News, July 22, 2021. Retrieved January 8, 2023, from https://psychnews.psychiatryonline.org/doi/10.1176/appi.pn.2021.7.14

Zhao, Y., *What Works May Hurt: Side Effects in Education,* Teachers College Press, 2018.

About the Author

Sean Slade is an Australian-American global education leader, speaker, and author, with three decades of experience in education across five countries and four continents. With a strong background in education reform and well-being, he has driven policy change, implemented initiatives, and developed educational leaders to enhance the social impact of education. He has helped lead the Whole Child movement in education, focusing on a more learner-centered and holistic approach to education, and has been a leading advocate for the alignment of health and education. A former teacher, head of department, and educational researcher, he serves as the head of BTS Spark, North America, a not-for-profit practice focusing on developing the next generation of school leaders. He is a Social & Emotional Learning expert for NBC Today, advisory member for the OECD's Future of Education & Skills 2030, hundrEd global ambassador, and a founding member of the UNESCO Chair on Global Health & Education. He has spoken around the world and written for numerous outlets, including the Washington Post, Huffington Post, and EdWeek and has been published by ASCD, Abingdon Press, Human Kinetics, and Routledge.

www.seantslade.com

www.ingramcontent.com/pod-product-compliance
Lightning Source LLC
Chambersburg PA
CBHW020749230426
43665CB00009B/542